D1528297

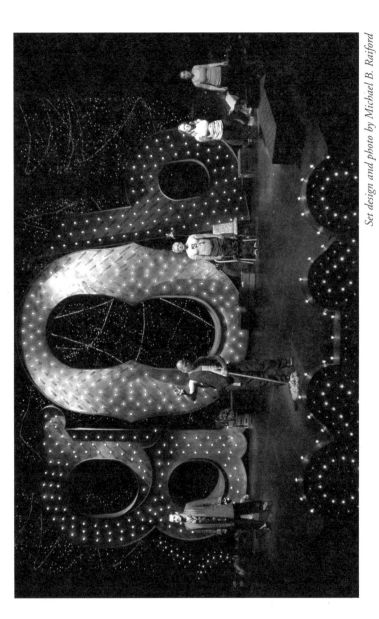

Set design and photo by Michael B. Raiford

Jeffrey Binder, Lou Sumrall, Danny Scheie, Polly Lee, and Aysan Celik in a scene from the Humana Festival production of *Bob: A Life in Five Acts*

BOB: A LIFE IN FIVE ACTS

BY PETER SINN NACHTRIEB

★

★

DRAMATISTS
PLAY SERVICE
INC.

SPECIAL NOTE

Originally commissioned and developed by South Coast Repertory.

BOB was developed with the support of Playwrights Foundation, San Francisco, (Amy L. Mueller, Artistic Director).

World premiere in the 2011 Humana Festival of New American Plays at ACTORS THEATRE LOUISVILLE.

For Bob

ACKNOWLEDGMENTS

BOB was commissioned and developed by South Coast Repertory.

BOB was developed with support of the Playwrights Foundation, San Francisco; Amy Mueller, Artistic Director.

THANKS TO: Sean Daniels for his creative brilliance and evangelism; Ken Prestininzi for once again being able to see into my brain; John Glore, Kelly Miller, Megan Monaghan, Sherri Butler-Hyner and everybody at SCR for birthing this play; Marc Masterson, Sarah Lunnie and everybody at ATL; Madeleine Oldham; Emily Schooltz and Ars Nova; Jonathan Spector, Amy Mueller, Lisa Steindler and the Z Space Studio, The National Theatre Conference, the Resident Playwrights of the Playwrights Foundation, Buck Busfield, Jerry Montoya and everyone at B Street Theatre, New Dramatists, Mark Orsini and Bruce Ostler and Bret Adams Ltd.

Kasey Mahaffy, Rob Nagle, Larry Bates, Angela Goethals, Blake Lindsley, Danny Wolohan, Arwen Anderson, Delia MacDougall, Nick Pelczar, Liam Vincent, Lance Gardner, Sally Dana, Matt Dellapina, Brett Robinson, David Turner, Jackie Viscusi, Joey DeChello, Ryan Barrentine, Brigette Davidovici, Lauren T. Mack, Dhyana Dahl, Kevin Tomlinson, Tyler Hastings, the Theatre Departments at FSU and UNLV, Jason Aaron Goldberg.

A special shout out to the fearless and wonderful souls that are Jeff Binder, Aysan Celik, Polly Lee, Danny Scheie, and Lou Sumrall. And to the Nachtrieb Family and Mark Marino for their love and awesomeness.

BOB: A LIFE IN FIVE ACTS received its world premiere at the Humana Festival at Actors Theatre of Louisville (Marc Masterson, Artistic Director) in Louisville, Kentucky, in March 2011. It was directed by Sean Daniels; the set design was by Michael B. Raiford; the costume design was by Lorraine Venberg; the lighting design was by Brian J. Lillenthal; the props design was by Joe Cunningham; the sound design was by Matt Callahan; and the production stage manager was Paul Mills Holmes. The cast was as follows:

BOB . . . . Jeffrey Binder
CHORUS ONE . . . . Aysan Celik
CHORUS TWO . . . . Lou Sumrall
CHORUS THREE . . . . Polly Lee
CHORUS FOUR . . . . Danny Scheie

CHARACTERS

BOB — from infant to old man. If handsome, unconventionally so. If not handsome, his personality adds something charismatic. Energy, optimism, open, active. American, of any or many cultural backgrounds.

THE CHORUS — Two women (Chorus One and Chorus Three) and two men (Chorus Two and Chorus Four). The chorus is, ideally, of unspecified but diverse cultural backgrounds. American. The Chorus will play themselves as well as every character in the play, aside from Bob. (See end of play for a possible breakdown of roles for each chorus member.) The Chorus is dispassionate but eloquent. The characters they assume are vivid, bright, sharp, and distinct. Even if they only have one line, there is pathos, history, and pain.

PLACE

All over the United States of America, interiors and exteriors. Plus one scene in Mexico. The play often changes rapidly from location to location and the shifts are quick. The speed of the changes is important and part of the ride of the play. My hunch is that the stagecraft in the play is exposed for being what it is.

TIME

From the birth to the death of Bob.

THE ACTS

ACT ONE — How Bob was born, abandoned, raised by a fast-food employee, discovers his dream, and almost dies.

ACT TWO — How Bob does not die, comes of age at a rest stop, pursues his dream, falls in love and has his heart broken.

ACT THREE — How Bob pursues his dream across America, gets chased out of many towns, meets an important man, and turns his back on everything he believed.

ACT FOUR — How Bob has a turn of luck, becomes a new man, achieves a false dream, meets an important woman and is redeemed.

ACT FIVE — The rest.

INTERLUDES

There are short interludes in between each act, each performed by a chorus member. I call them "dances" in the play but they could be any sort of brief performance with no words.

An intermission is perhaps best placed between Acts Three and Four.

MUSIC

Yes. Underscoring. Maybe a live musician. Maybe the Chorus plays music.

MOOD

Epic, cinematic, a whirlwind, a ride.

BOB: A LIFE
IN FIVE ACTS

ACT ONE

The Chorus enters.

ALL CHORUS. Bob. A life in five acts.
CHORUS ONE. Act One.
CHORUS TWO. How Bob is born, abandoned, raised by a fast-food employee, discovers his dream, and almost dies. *(A sterile fast-food restaurant bathroom. Chorus Three assumes the character of Helen. She is sweating, crying, breathing heavy, legs wide.)*
CHORUS ONE. It is said that Bob was born on Valentine's Day in the bathroom of a White Castle Restaurant in Louisville, Kentucky. It is said that Bob's birth mother, whose name was Helen, was feeling particularly lonely and depressed on this holiday and felt that only a certain cuisine would soothe her ache.
CHORUS TWO. It is said that Helen was unaware of the Valentine's Day tradition of the usually more subdued restaurant to adorn their tables with candles and cloths and other romantic miscellany and that the restaurant would be packed with couples flaunting their couplehood.
CHORUS FOUR. Nor was Helen aware of how severe her physiological reaction would be to witnessing this vast scene of public love until, after eating much faster than she intended, she rushed into the bathroom, pushed to urinate and her wombic fluids erupted onto the bathroom floor. *(Wombic fluids erupt out of Helen.)*
CHORUS ONE. Nor was she aware how quickly labor could be sometimes until five minutes after her water broke, Bob would

emerge quickly and fiercely from her magic chamber. *(A pop. Baby Bob flies out of Helen, umbilical cord attached.)*

CHORUS TWO. Nor did she expect the emotional response she would have to this birth … a progression from joy to relief to memories to regret to fear to terror to anger to hatred to wanting absolutely nothing to do with what had just emerged. *(Helen pulls out a knife.)*

CHORUS FOUR. She did remember the small sign posted outside the restaurant below the "Meal Deal" poster: the blue outline of a house, silhouette of an infant sitting in large comforting hands, "Safe Place" written in multiple languages below. At that moment, Helen made a decision that would ultimately affect thousands of lives. *(Helen takes the umbilical cord, cuts it with the knife.)*

CHORUS TWO. It is said that this was the only advice Helen could think to give her newborn son.

HELEN. Good luck. *(Helen runs off.)*

CHORUS FOUR. This is what Bob did when he was alone. *(Bob assesses the situation.)*

BOB. BWAHHH! *(Jeanine, a White Castle employee, enters the bathroom.)*

JEANINE. Oh my.

CHORUS THREE. Her name was Jeanine. This is how Jeanine saved Bob. *(Lights Shift. By the counter. Jeanine, holding Bob, reads corporate instructions on a piece of paper.)*

JEANINE. *(Reading.)* Step one: Retrieve baby/child and take him/her/it to a neutral yet safe space behind the service counter. *(Jeanine moves.)* Do not stand near fryers. *(Jeanine moves again.)* Step two: Determine if parent or guardian is still on the property. *(Jeanine takes counter microphone.)* Attention Valentine's Day guests. We hope you are all enjoying your romantic meals. If there is anyone in the restaurant who may have left a personal item in the bathroom, would you please come to the counter at this time? *(Jeanine waits.)* Step three: Should no one claim baby/child, immediately phone the police, Child Protective Services, and the corporate legal crisis line. Under no circumstances should you look into the baby's eyes and fall in love with it. Do not fall in love with the baby. *(Jeanine lowers the paper. Jeanine tries to not look at Bob. Jeanine looks at Bob. Jeanine falls in love with Bob.)*

CHORUS FOUR. This is why Jeanine decided to raise Bob as her own. *(Jeanine driving, Bob in a bundle next to her.)*

10

JEANINE. I was finishing up my Sunday night dinner at the Bamboo Wok. I don't know how authentic or healthy it is but I like the flavors. I'd been working my way through the menu for about a year. Each week, I would have a new entrée in order of appearance. I'd finally made it to the "Noodles slash Rice" section after several months of Lamb and I felt like I was entering a new era in my life. When the waiter delivered the check and cookie, the fortune inside seemed different. The paper looked shiny, almost golden, the ink darker, more insistent.

FORTUNE COOKIE VOICE (CHORUS TWO). "You will be the mother to a great great man."

JEANINE. The fortunes I usually get are a little more vague than that. But this felt intentional. Like someone was watching me. From inside the cookie.

FORTUNE COOKIE VOICE (CHORUS TWO). "You will be the mother to a great great man."

JEANINE. It made me smile. I thought, "Well, cool, Jeanine, maybe the future isn't only selling tiny burgers and having Asian food once a week." And then my stomach started to twitch, felt like I was gonna be sick. I started sweating, breathing heavy. And I thought, Oh my god, it's happening already. I stood up from my table and shouted "I'm gonna be the mother to a great great man!" Next thing I knew I woke up in a hospital bed. At first I thought I'd conceived my great man immaculate till the nurse told me that I'd almost died at the restaurant. That I had a severe reaction to the gluten in Asian noodles slash rice that messed up my insides so much that I would never be able to make a "great great man" the regular way. I don't really care for fortunes very much anymore. But, funny, you know, there you are. There you are. I must be just a weird noise in your ear. You little moving thing. I will give you food and shelter. I will educate you. I will make sure that becoming President of the United States remains a possibility. Even if it kills me, I will make you a great great man. *(Shift.)*

CHORUS FOUR. This is how Bob got his name. *(Jeanine's house. Bonnie, Jeanine's friend, is there. Jeanine is playing with Bob. Bonnie stares at Jeanine. Bob is examining.)*

BONNIE. You don't look exhausted.

JEANINE. I'm not exhausted, Bonnie.

BONNIE. Trust me. In a few days you will be exhausted for the rest of your life.

JEANINE. He sleeps through the night.

BONNIE. Since when?

JEANINE. Since I got him five days ago.

BONNIE. I read that babies who sleep through the night often have learning disabilities. It was in *Newsweek*.

BOB. Ghshablah.

JEANINE. What should I name him?

BONNIE. You don't have a name for him yet?

JEANINE. It's not like I got to plan ahead for this. *(Bonnie starts to cry.)* Bonnie?

BONNIE. Are you sure you can do this?

JEANINE. I think so.

BONNIE. The choices you make right now will determine a life of joy or a life of pain.

BOB. Ooo.

JEANINE. It's just a name, Bonnie.

BONNIE. THE NAME IS EVERYTHING, JEANINE! First impressions, schoolyard happiness, entire futures depend on the name. I read that in *Newsweek* too. This is a child's future. THINK OF THE FUTURE.

JEANINE. You're getting a little angry, Bonnie.

BONNIE. I was given the wrong name! Someone asks, "What's your name?" and I say "Bonnie" and people think something's wrong with me 'cause I don't seem very "Bonnie-like." I'm suspect from the get-go and that ripples and ripples, a chain reaction against my favor and look at me now. If I wasn't "Bonnie," I'd be a different person. I'd have a better life. I wouldn't want to die. Chester. *(Bonnie does a flourish with her hands. Exits.)*

JEANINE. What do you think? If you could be called anything in the world, what would it be?

BOB. Bwahhhhhhhhhhhh. *(Beat.)*

JEANINE. What was that?

BABY BOB. Argh baplbbbtss urgglmmmmmmm … bwaahhbb.

JEANINE. Did you just say —

BABY BOB. Bwaahb.

JEANINE. Bob? Bob. Bob. Bob.

BABY BOB. Bwahb. *(Jeanine looks out — a thought to the future. The Chorus each take alternating lines.)*

CHORUS TWO. Welcome our newest student, Bob.

CHORUS THREE. What a beautiful painting, Bob.

CHORUS FOUR. You were just incredible at recess, Bob.

CHORUS TWO. Bob the way you play hockey, I don't know what to feel.

CHORUS THREE. Kiss me Bob.

CHORUS FOUR. Here, take this special chair, Bob.

CHORUS TWO. Bob you can be anything you want.

CHORUS THREE. Be a historian, Bob.

CHORUS FOUR. Be an artist, Bob.

CHORUS TWO. Cure, Bob. Cure the sick.

CHORUS THREE. Kiss me again Bob.

CHORUS FOUR. Bob, kiss us both at the same time.

CHORUS TWO. I love you Bob.

CHORUS THREE. I love You Bob.

CHORUS FOUR. Bob must be stopped.

JEANINE. Bob. Your name is Bob.

BABY BOB. Bwahb. *(A banging on the door.)*

CONNOR. Open up, Jeanine!

CHORUS FOUR. This is why Jeanine decided to leave town with Bob.

JEANINE. That's the police, Bob. *(A bang.)*

CONNOR. Jeanine!

JEANINE. It's open! Stay quiet, Bob.

BABY BOB. Bwahb.

JEANINE. Stay quiet. *(Jeanine hides Bob in a grocery bag. Connor, a police officer, enters.)*

CONNOR. Jeanine.

JEANINE. Connor.

BABY BOB. Bwahb.

CONNOR. Been a long time.

JEANINE. Seen you around.

CONNOR. It's been a long time. *(The pain of their history is felt.)*

JEANINE. How can I help you, Connor?

CONNOR. You still working at the White Castle?

JEANINE. You know I still work there.

CONNOR. Anything weird happen the last few days?

JEANINE. Something weird happens every day. Our lighting has a way of pushing people over the edge.

CONNOR. We got a call at the station today.

JEANINE. Well, good for you.

CONNOR. Some woman.

JEANINE. Of course it was a woman.

CONNOR. Crying. Didn't say her name. Just asked if "he was OK."

JEANINE. Who?

CONNOR. She wouldn't say. Said she "had to do it," that "if I knew the whole story," blah de blah and I had to interrupt: "Ma'am, what you are talking about?" She said, "White Castle" and hung up.

JEANINE. How odd.

CONNOR. Anyone leave an infant at the White Castle on Valentine's Day?

BOB. Bwahb.

JEANINE. Not to my recollection.

CONNOR. You've always had a great memory.

JEANINE. Don't butter me, Connor.

CONNOR. I'm just saying you have a tendency of not forgetting any and all things that happen.

JEANINE. I like to learn from my mistakes. *(Beat.)*

CONNOR. I've seen you at the Bamboo Wok.

JEANINE. Don't.

CONNOR. Eating alone every week.

JEANINE. I enjoy self-dining.

CONNOR. Maybe I can join you sometime.

JEANINE. Connor, thank you for your diligent police work but alas, I do not recollect anyone leaving a Bob at my place of employment.

CONNOR. A what?

BOB. Bob.

JEANINE. A baby.

CONNOR. You said Bob.

JEANINE. I meant a baby.

BOB. Bobby.

CONNOR. Who's Bob? *(Bob pokes his head out.)*

JEANINE. It's someone I'm seeing. His name is Bob. *(Beat.)*

CONNOR. I don't believe it.

JEANINE. I fell in love with him the moment I saw him.

CONNOR. What does Bob do?

BOB. Bob do. Do Bob Bob.

JEANINE. He is a great great man.

BOB. Gray. Man.

CONNOR. I guess it was a mistake to come here. *(Connor almost exits, turns.)* I want you back, Jeanine. I want another chance.

JEANINE. You had your chance, Connor. *(Beat.)*

CONNOR. If you see anything at work —
JEANINE. Nothing would overjoy me more. *(Connor almost exits, turns.)*
CONNOR. One day, Jeanine Bordeaux, I will prove myself to you. *(Connor exits.)*
BOB. Bwahb. Proo Mah Salf.
JEANINE. We can't stay here, Bob.
CHORUS FOUR. It is said that Jeanine collected the few belongings she felt to be essential, including a pillowcase filled with her life savings, and left her home forever to raise Bob in her beige Chevy Malibu. This is the road trip of Bob and Jeanine. *(A "road trip" that spans twelve years. The Chorus assists.)*
JEANINE. That is the sky. That's a tree. Black walnut. That's a dead goat. That's a fire. You'll want to be careful with that. *(White Castle.)* That's where I worked. *(Las Vegas.)* That's where they play roulette. *(A religious sign asking "Where you will spend eternity?")* That's a good question. *(Bamboo Wok.)* Don't eat there. That's a farmer. That's someone who delivers things to people. That one's crazy. And that one's evil. *(The Grand Canyon.)* This is the Grand Canyon, Bob.
BOB. Whoa.
JEANINE. It was carved by the Colorado River over millions of years. And it's still changing. *(Pointing.)* As are those Rocky Mountains, those mesas, this coastline. The ground beneath us is undergoing constant change, Bob.
BOB. Erosion. *(A house in South Carolina.)*
JEANINE. And it was here that they would rest, but only for a few hours. Danger was always close. Nineteen times Ms. Tubman made this journey. That's what you do when things aren't right, Bob.
BOB. Railroad. *(New Mexico.)*
JEANINE. And it was here that Mr. Oppenheimer dropped his experiment from a wooden tower and fission ensued. One event can change the world, Bob.
BOB. Chain reaction. *(The first Wal-Mart.)*
JEANINE. And it was here that Mr. Walton opened the first stores that ushered in a new type of shopping experience. But he still always drove the same old truck, Bob.
BOB. Entrepreneur. *(Mt. Rushmore.)*
JEANINE. And even though Lincoln was killed at a play, the decisions he made would change the course of our nation. One man can change everything.

BOB. So if I do something amazing, someone else will carve my face onto a mountain?

JEANINE. There are lots of factors involved when getting put on a mountain. Politics. Popularity. Your face. A lot of achievements go completely unrecognized, not even on a plaque.

BOB. What's a plaque? *(They look at a plaque.)*

JEANINE. It's a marker, Bob. To pay tribute to some great act or person.

BOB. *(Rubbing fingers over letters.)* "In Memory of Great Sculptor Gutzon Borglum." It's beautiful.

JEANINE. And they last forever.

BOB. I want to be on a plaque someday.

JEANINE. Well, you can be, Bob.

BOB. In memory of Bob, the man who rescued a town from destruction! Bob, the great entertainer and tamer of beasts. Bob, the man who invented a blanket you can wear!

JEANINE. You better keep a piece of paper handy to write all your ideas down.

BOB. I've got some paper in my pocket!

JEANINE. You can do anything you want with your life, Bob.

BOB. You should be on a plaque, Mom.

JEANINE. Oh, Bob, that's, well, that's the nicest thing anyone has ever —

BOB. Let's go.

JEANINE. We don't always have to be in such a rush.

BOB. But Mom, if I am to become great, there is so much I have to learn and see! *(The montage goes into overdrive. Bob's energy remains high. The trip is killing Jeanine.)*

BOB. Birthplaces!

JEANINE. Battlegrounds.

BOB. Big cities!

JEANINE. Empty stretches.

BOB. Public parks

JEANINE. Private islands.

BOB. Man-made lakes.

JEANINE. Hoover Dams.

BOB. Holy sites.

JEANINE. Corn Palaces.

BOB. Dinosaur bones.

JEANINE. Swinger camps.

BOB. Monuments.
JEANINE. Junkyards.
BOB. Luxury homes.
JEANINE. Trailer parks.
BOB. Ham and Cheese omelets.
JEANINE. Coffee.
BOB. More Ham and Cheese omelets.
JEANINE. Indigestion.
BOB. Fudge.
JEANINE. Ibuprofen.
BOB. Art and science
JEANINE. Wow that is hurting —
BOB. History and Civics
JEANINE. Can't quite —
BOB. Beauty and Truth —
JEANINE. catch my breath —
BOB. Knowledge and Experience!
JEANINE. *(In pain.)* Too much to experience. *(Chicago. Bob is 12. Jeanine is ill.)*
BOB. C'mon, the museum closes at four so we need to —
JEANINE. I can't seem to catch my breath, Bob.
BOB. They're not gonna let us in!
JEANINE. Maybe we can go tomorrow.
BOB. No, I want to see the canvasses now. The brushstrokes with which Grant Wood captured the gothic soul of an elderly couple, the splatters of Pollock that drip anguish and liquor, the flowers of O'Keefe that evoke the beauty of nature and vaginas at the same time.
JEANINE. My, Bob, you soak everything up like a roll of Bounty.
BOB. Moving from place to place, collecting visitor guides and souvenir spoons, learning trigonometry as we eat ham and cheese omelets … I love everything we do together, Mom.
JEANINE. I'm not your real mother, Bob.
BOB. What?
JEANINE. You were left at the White Castle. I wasn't supposed to take you. But then I looked into your eyes.
BOB. You did?
JEANINE. Most people don't grow up in Malibus. They don't drive around the country with all their money in a pillowcase.
BOB. That's because we're special.

JEANINE. You, Bob, are a special special boy.

BOB. You're making me blush. *(Jeanine collapses.)* Are you OK?

JEANINE. There's a bit of money left in the bag, Bob. You're going to have to use it wisely.

BOB. You're soaking wet.

JEANINE. Keep an eye out for danger and advantage-takers. Don't skimp on oil changes for the Malibu. And always wear your undies.

BOB. What is happening right now?

JEANINE. I'm dying, Bob.

BOB. No, you're not.

JEANINE. My liver is pressing out, cracking my ribs. It's getting harder to breathe. I want to blame those Bamboo Wok noodles that combo cursed and blessed me years ago but I think it just happened. You know how things just happen.

BOB. I'll call an ambulance.

JEANINE. Don't.

BOB. Ambulance!

JEANINE. It's too late, Bob.

BOB. Phineas Gage survived a metal rod through his head. Lance Armstrong survived cancer to win the Tour de France. Dean Martin lived till he was seventy-eight.

JEANINE. Look at you trying to do something. You're twelve years old and you're already a man.

BOB. I don't want to be.

JEANINE. Well in a second, Bob, I'm going to breathe my last breath and then I'm going to slump over and my body may twitch but I'll be gone. My heat will drain, but if you hug me it'll drain into you. After that happens, I want you to light me on fire. Gather some flammables, lay me on top, and set me on fire.

BOB. I'm going to get on the plaque for the both of us, Mom.

JEANINE. It's Jeanine. I love you, Bob.

BOB. I love you too, Jeanine.

JEANINE. Good luck. *(Bob hugs Jeanine. Jeanine dies. Bob puts Jeanine down. He gathers a few sticks, newspaper and other burning supplies, puts them under Jeanine. Bob lights a match, drops it on the ground. A police siren. Bob and Connor, who is now a Chicago Policeman, at an interrogation table.)*

CHORUS FOUR. This is how Bob avoided prison.

CONNOR. You do realize it's illegal to cremate someone on the steps of the Art Institute of Chicago.

BOB. It's what she wanted.

CONNOR. There are concerns. About pollution. Asthma.

BOB. I don't care so long as she's everywhere.

CONNOR. And now we can't do an autopsy. We'll never get to know what caused her death.

BOB. She said some things just happen.

CONNOR. That's not good enough for the paperwork. Was she dead before you lit her on fire?

BOB. YES!

CONNOR. OK, OK. It's required we ask that.

BOB. I don't know what it's going to be like without her.

CONNOR. It's going to suck, probably. There's going to be a lot of people you lose in your life. Some die. Some move away. Some you just say the wrong thing to. You'll have those days. When you'll be so sad, praying you could just see her even for an instant before she vanishes into a puff of smoke.

BOB. Do you have any more Kleenex? *(Connor gives a Kleenex to Bob.)*

CONNOR. Well, since there's no one to claim you, we may have to put you in prison till this all gets straightened out.

BOB. No. I have to learn about airports tomorrow!

CONNOR. It's a prison for kids, so it's not so gloomy.

BOB. I have a lot of great things to do with my life!

CONNOR. Well, you're not allowed to do that. Not till you're eighteen, uh, what is your name?

BOB. Bob. My name is Bob.

OTHER CHORUS. *(Whisper.)* Bob!

CONNOR. Why does that name haunt me?

BOB. It was my first word.

CONNOR. Where were you born?

BOB. In a White Castle.

OTHER CHORUS. *(Whisper, unsuccessfully in unison.)* White Castle.

CONNOR. What was the name of the woman you just burnt?

BOB. Jeanine. Her name was Jeanine. *(Connor drops his pen.)*

CONNOR. Oh my. Oh my oh my oh my.

BOB. You dropped your pen. *(Connor gets on one knee, pulls out a ring.)*

CONNOR. I was going to give this to her the next time I saw her. I've had this in my pocket for eleven years. I said, "Connor, even if you're in a bathroom stall mid-tinkle and you see her, get on your knees ASAP and beg her to come back." *(Connor grabs Bob's hand, perhaps kissing the soot of Jeanine in Bob's hand.)* Oh my sweet Slider Highness ... I'm sorry for being selfish and stupid. I'm sorry for making you so sad on the day you looked the prettiest. *(Connor gives Bob the ring.)*

BOB. This would have looked beautiful on her finger.

CONNOR. Keep it somewhere safe. It's a dangerous world out there. Keep it in your undies. I think I'm going to go back to the museum and, just breathe awhile. Good luck, Bob. *(Connor exits. Bob is alone.)*

BOB. Hello? *(Bob looks at the ring. He puts it in his undies and steps outdoors into the cold Chicago air.)* You're on your own, Bob. On West Monroe Street, Chicago. *(A gust of wind.)* The "Windy City." Home of the White Sox, late-night sketch comedy, and the "fresheezie": a hot dog wrapped in bacon and filled with American cheese ... a meal that is delightful and cruel at the same time. At the Alamo, the Texans were outnumbered, but they were able to fight off the Mexican Army twice before they all got killed. In the Sierra Nevada, trapped by snow and bad teamwork, the Donner Party withstood bitter cold and the sour taste of human flesh for seven of them to survive and reach the state of California. "You can do anything you want with your life." So said Jeanine Bordeaux, the safest driver and best breakfast companion ever. And today I'm going to get in our Malibu that should be parked right here and ... *(A citizen walks by.)* Excuse me, businessperson, have you seen a Malibu that was parked here? *(The citizen ignores Bob. Another citizen runs by, avoiding eye contact.)* Hello there, forlorn woman, did you happen to see what happened to a Malibu that was here? *(A citizen walks by, the pillowcase slung over his/her back and scurries off.)* There was a pillowcase with wet kittens on tugboats under the passenger seat ... *(Bob takes a step. His shoe breaks.)* My shoe. *(Helen, Bob's birth mother and now a thief, runs in with her knife.)*

HELEN. Give me your shirt!

BOB. What?

HELEN. Give me your shirt before I cut your face! NOW! *(Bob removes his shirt, gives it to Helen.)*

BOB. What are you doing with my shirt?

HELEN. Are you wearing underwear?

BOB. That's private.

HELEN. ARE YOU WEARING UNDERWEAR?

BOB. I always do!

HELEN. Then give me your pants.

BOB. Jeanine bought me these pants at the Rock and Roll Hall of Fame. Please, my name is Bob and —

HELEN. WELL MY NAME IS HELEN!

CHORUS. *(Whispering.)* Helen.

HELEN. GIVE ME YOUR ROCK AND ROLL PANTS AND YOU'LL LIVE ANOTHER DAY ON THIS CURS-ED EARTH. *(Bob removes his pants, gives them to Helen. Helen looks into Bob's eyes. An echo.)* If only you knew what has driven me to this ... Good luck. *(Helen runs off.)*

BOB. Good luck. *(Bob walks against the wind, exits. Blackout.)*

End of Act One

Interlude 1

A dance about hardship.

CHORUS THREE. This is my dance about hardship. *(Chorus Three dances.)* Thank you.

ACT TWO

ALL CHORUS. Bob. Act Two.

CHORUS THREE. How Bob does not die, comes of age at a rest stop, pursues his dream, falls in love and has his heart broken. *(The sound of brakes and tires skidding. Bob is lying on the ground. Seth, a trucker, holds a bag of trash. Seth kicks Bob.)*

SETH. You need to move.

BOB. Wh — What?

SETH. You need-o to move-o your body-o.

BOB. Where am I?

SETH. Boy, you are face-down in a large vehicle parking spot. On the pavement. Where bodies should not lay.

BOB. Am I dead?

SETH. You're conscious, you're talking, so dead you are not. But I almost ran you over with my Rocky Mountain Double and if that'd happened, well, you'd be a flapjack and I'd be devastated. *(Seth dumps his bag into a trashcan.)*

BOB. This scary woman named Helen stole my pants and I was crying and walking along the interstate and I don't remember how —

SETH. "Just say no," boy.

BOB. No. What?

SETH. I quote you the immortal words of Nancy Reagan. I lost two children to the stuff. One's dead to me and the other one's dead. Every part of my past hurts so I've turned to God and the road. A little prayer and air on my face and I'm just starting to enjoy the warmth of the sun and you almost bescuttled the whole effort so for the love of Jesus and Literal Seven-Day Creation BE CAREFUL WHERE YOU SLEEP! *(Seth exits. Bob pulls himself up, sees a sign in the distance.)*

BOB. William Burroughs Memorial Rest Stop. Mound City, Missouri. 550 miles from Chicago. How did I get here? *(Perhaps with a reenactment.)*

CHORUS ONE. It is said that Bob fell unconscious during his walk out of Chicago and fell into the back of a Honda Civic owned by Jeanine's friend Bonnie who had recently left her hometown in search of a new name. Bonnie had pulled to the side of the road and

23

raised the trunk to prevent other drivers from seeing her urinate on her birth certificate in a ceremonial ritual of transition to a new life. Bonnie discovered Bob when she re-opened her trunk at the William Burroughs Memorial Rest Stop where she pulled him out.

BOB. Jeanine used to pull out a Snickers from her purse every time we hit a snag, like when there was four hours of traffic to get to Hoover Dam, when I got a B on a chemistry test, or when we got to the Michelle Kwan Museum and it was closed for renovation. I could really use a Snickers right now. *(Bob walks to Seth's trash bag and begins to look through it.)* Water. One eighth of a cheeseburger. Seven Pringles. This note is legal tender. *(Turns it sideways, reading a scrawl.)* Barry Metcalf is a slut. Bloody shirt. Rubber gloves. Knife. *(Condoms.)* Balloons! *The Grapes of Wrath* by John Steinbeck. *The Adventures of Huckleberry Finn* by Mark Twain. *The Long Road Home* by Danielle Steel. *(Finds a Snickers wrapper.)* Jackpot. "Pick stuff up from the ground and make something." The great semi-accessible combinalist Robert Rauschenberg said that. And be careful where you sleep. *(Bob gets dressed in a bizarre outfit, each piece reflecting a different person's fashion.)*

CHORUS ONE. It is said that Bob built his shelter in a gulch behind the rest stop lavatories that nobody seemed to notice. He kept himself fed, clean, warm, and occupied himself with fitness, foraging, self-cleaning, reading, and writing.

BOB. Dear Bob's Diary: Four thousand twenty-three people passed through the W.B.M.R.S. today. Of those travelers, four came up and talked to me. *(James, a middle-aged Bear [Chorus Two].)*

JAMES. I'm James.

BOB. Today I met James. Brand-new RV.

JAMES. I was living in Florida.

BOB. Oo the Everglades!

JAMES. Felt like a sticky bun whole time I was there. But Roberto, *mi oso novio*, he loved it. Met him at this very rest stop many years ago. Got so lost in his eyes the itchiness of the shrub we were under hardly made an impression. He's gone now. 'Gator caught my Bear skinny-dipping. Roberto put up quite a fight but it'd been a while since he'd been to the gym. I've come to spread his ashes on the bush where we met. I could mourn forever but 'Berto'd hate me for it so I've burnt our house down, used the insurance money to buy that RV, and I plan on having enough sex in public places for the both of us.

BOB. Lesson: Live for the dead. Don't mourn forever. Honor the bushes. *(Caitlyn, sorority sister [Chorus One].)*
CAITLYN. *(Intense relief.)* I almost didn't make it!
BOB. Caitlyn. Volkswagen Cabriolet.
CAITLYN. I've had to go for like a hundred miles!
BOB. Go where?
CAITLYN. Frikkin' forty-eight ounce ice tea. Stupid, Caitlyn!
BOB. You are stupid, Caitlyn!
CAITLYN. But I made it. I breathed deep and I sang and I cried and I texted my friends and I clenched and I saw the darkness but I made it I made it and I was seriously peeing for like two minutes. Wooooooo! Woooooooooooo!
BOB. Lesson: You can make it if you clench. *(Kim, little girl [Chorus Three].)*
KIM. Do you have a pencil?
BOB. Kim, 1988 windowless Dodge Van. *(Bob gives Kim a pencil.)*
KIM. I met that damp man over there in the Rainforest Cafe parking lot a week ago. He said get in, and I got in. I realize now that was a mistake and now I understand why the rule my mom told me exists. I s'pose I could just ask someone to help set me free, but then I wouldn't learn. As my daddy said when I spilt pudding on the floor: "You made the mess, you clean it up." So I'm waiting for the perfect moment to stab his neck with a pencil and get home to my mom and dad. Thank you.
BOB. Lesson: Always have a pencil. *(Sagé, Burning Man hippie [Chorus Four].)*
SAGÉ. We're like a thousand human fleas —
BOB. Sagé. School bus covered with metal spirals and beach glass.
SAGÉ. And this rest stop is like a wolf. And we have all gathered in its fur to relax and share stories. A hundred million years from now, the world is going to be how it is because we were here. Hopping. And hopping. And —
BOB. Not everyone has a lesson. But everyone has a mission! *(Chorus as other travelers.)*
MERTLE (CHORUS ONE). I'm bringin' pot roast to my son locked in prison.
VIJAY (CHORUS TWO). I sell Indian food from the back of my Jeep.
SALMON (CHORUS THREE). I'm raising awareness of the Prairie Mole Cricket.

WAYNE (CHORUS FOUR). I bring cocaine and cheap labor to greater Wisconsin.
BOB. Everyone has a hero!
CHORUS ONE. I want to be like Michael Jordan.
CHORUS TWO. I want to be like Hillary Rodham Clinton.
CHORUS THREE. I want to be like Harvey Milk.
CHORUS FOUR. I want to be like Joseph Smith.
CHORUS ONE. Hester Prynne.
CHORUS TWO. Jack Bauer.
CHORUS THREE. Holden Caulfield.
CHORUS FOUR. Buffy the Vampire Slayer.
JAMES. Roberto.
KIM. My daddy.
CAITLYN. My bladder.
SAGÉ. Hop hop.
BOB. I am going to be a hero for someone. *(Showing his list.)* My list of great ideas is growing longer and stronger every day. So much I can do and this is where it begins, Bob's diary. I can make this the greatest rest stop in the country. I'll clean the bathrooms every other hour. I'll carve better trails into the hills and tidy the bushes where the men meet their soulmates. Late at night, using paint left by the trash, I will reconfigure the parking design to foster a greater sense of community amongst the travelers. Bob, rest stop maverick. The Bob Memorial Rest Stop. Put it on a plaque. Do you think when someone reads your name on a plaque hundreds of years after you're dead, for a brief instant, you exist again? All of a sudden the patch of mushrooms, the bit of that tree, that soil or dust that were once your molecules suddenly experience a moment of connectedness, a memory of their past teamwork as being part of a human being that did something that was so important it had to be recognized. On a plaque.
CHORUS THREE. It is said that in the years that Bob lived at the William Burroughs Memorial Rest Stop near Mound City, Missouri, it became the most cared-for stop in the country.
CHORUS FOUR. It is said that the reputation of the facility spread among the traveling community, even gaining special mention in *Lonely Planet Missouri.*
CHORUS ONE. It is said that people who stopped in did indeed feel more rested.
CHORUS TWO. Six years passed.

CHORUS THREE. New chemicals began to course through Bob's body.

BOB. *(Slightly deeper voice.)* Hello there. *(Bob's body changes. More adult.)*

CHORUS FOUR. Bob's body began to change. Thicker, stronger.

BOB. Oh wow, new hair.

CHORUS FOUR. Bob became a man. *(Bob has a surprising orgasm.)*

BOB. I am a man!

CHORUS ONE. It is said that Bob felt love for this place.

BOB. I love this rest stop.

CHORUS TWO. Bob felt love for many things.

BOB. I love my shelter. I love this table. I love my books.

CHORUS TWO. But this is how Bob fell in love for the first and only time. *(Amelia, radiant and urgent, walks in and kisses Bob on the lips. While they kiss, she takes a picture with a Polaroid instant camera. Amelia exits. Amelia returns.)*

AMELIA. What's your name?

BOB. Bwahhh. Bob. *(Amelia writes Bob's name down.)*

AMELIA. You're a good kisser, Bob.

BOB. I've never kissed anyone before.

AMELIA. Then you're a natural.

BOB. Oh well I don't know if I'mmrrfruhljsakj. *(Amelia exits.)* Hey! *(Amelia returns.)* What's your name?

AMELIA. Amelia.

BOB. Like the aviatrix?

AMELIA. That's who I was named after.

BOB. She broke barriers. She was a vanguard. And then she disappeared.

AMELIA. That's my favorite part about her. The mystery. She wanted to go where nobody would find her.

BOB. Into the ocean?

AMELIA. Or maybe she found a place she could hide. *(Amelia almost exits.)*

BOB. Could we do that again?

AMELIA. Kiss?

BOB. I would like to very much.

AMELIA. That's not on the list.

BOB. You have a list?

AMELIA. "One kiss with a stranger at a rest stop." I've got a thousand things I have to do before I get home.

BOB. I've got a list too!

AMELIA. You do? *(Bob pulls out his list.)*

BOB. I write down every idea of what I'd like to accomplish with my life: Create defensive knives for children in danger. Design ornaments that widows can hang on their lover's bushes. Cure diseases that suddenly kill people on steps of museums.

AMELIA. *(Pulling out her list.)* See an old-growth redwood forest in the nude. Do a shot of tequila with an on-duty policeman. Fill a jar with water from the Pacific Ocean.

BOB. Your list is fun.

AMELIA. Yours is long.

BOB. I'm only 18.

AMELIA. Are you in high school or college?

BOB. Jeanine, who raised me but was my false mother, taught me a whole lot before I set her on fire. I made a promise that I'll become a great man.

AMELIA. You may need to go to college to do that.

BOB. Sean John Puffy Combs didn't finish college. Jimmy Dean, Sausage King, didn't finish high school. Nor did Ansel Adams. Or Grover Cleveland. Or Walt Disney. Thomas Edison.

AMELIA. You have a point.

BOB. I like your hair. *(Beat.)*

AMELIA. I'm getting married this summer.

BOB. Oh. Congratulations.

AMELIA. My parents set it up. They're big into lineage, having a marriage "mean something" on a historical and financial level. And Chet, that's actually his name, is the perfect match. He's the son of a CEO, and I'm the daughter of a CEO, and our union will restore peace to the corporate community. But I don't love him.

BOB. That doesn't sound like a very good marriage.

AMELIA. I told my parents that I would be miserable with Chet and they told me not to be selfish.

BOB. That's terrible.

AMELIA. I insisted that if I go ahead with it that I needed to leave town on my own for a trip around the country where I could celebrate my final moments of happiness. I asked fifty friends and family to come up with a list of things they think I should do before the big day. They all came up with twenty. One thousand final acts. I've got three months.

BOB. We don't have a lot of time.

AMELIA. Where are you heading?

BOB. Just collecting some trash for an evening fire.

AMELIA. You live here?

BOB. Mostly behind the bathrooms. Check out my flat! *(Bob's shelter is revealed.)*

AMELIA. Oh my.

BOB. See all the neck pillows?

AMELIA. Your own little hideout.

BOB. And I have books!

AMELIA. You know I can give you a ride somewhere. Some money.

BOB. I don't want to leave.

AMELIA. You're happy.

BOB. I am right now. Hey, I just remembered another idea from my list. *(Reading list.)* Get second kiss from girl soon to be married.

AMELIA. You just made that up.

BOB. Does that matter? *(Amelia smiles. Bob kisses Amelia. It's really good.)*

AMELIA. You've never kissed anyone before?

BOB. No.

AMELIA. That could be your legacy.

BOB. People aren't celebrated for being great kissers.

AMELIA. Burt Lancaster. Clark Gable. Charo.

BOB. You're really pretty.

AMELIA. I've got to go.

BOB. You're the most beautiful girl with a list I've ever seen. *(Amelia cries.)* I didn't mean to —

AMELIA. I just wish I could do what I want.

BOB. You can do anything you want with your life, Amelia.

AMELIA. That's a slogan for shoes, Bob. We all have constraints. Limits to what we can do.

BOB. Some of the greatest people in our country fought limits. Helen Keller fought the limits of her senses. Madonna fought the limits of her voice.

AMELIA. I think that's why you're such a good kisser.

BOB. What?

AMELIA. I can taste the optimism on your lips.

BOB. You do?

AMELIA. In your spit. It's sweet.

BOB. Someone just left a whole chicken on a picnic table this morning. It still smells good. We can roast it over a trash fire and watch the sun set over the interstate.

AMELIA. My list …

BOB. I have a really large bed made with Kleenex.

AMELIA. I can't ignore my life.

BOB. This can be your hideout. Amelia's Island. *(Beat.)*

AMELIA. Would you make love to me?

BOB. With what?

AMELIA. You'll figure it out.

BOB. I've only heard it in the parking lot.

AMELIA. Just let me taste that hope again. *(They kiss and fall to the ground.)*

CHORUS ONE. It is said that Bob and Amelia made love for fourteen hours on Bob's bed made of Kleenex.

CHORUS FOUR. It is said that it was the best lovemaking Bob and Amelia would ever experience. Way better than Chet.

CHORUS ONE. Amelia stayed with Bob at the rest stop for two weeks, making love for most of the day, taking breaks to sleep, giggle or forage for food from the trash bins.

CHORUS FOUR. For a post-coital moment, Amelia thought she might like to stay there forever. Until in the middle of one night, Bob said this.

BOB. Stay with me forever.

AMELIA. Oh Bob.

BOB. I don't want this to end.

AMELIA. What about your list?

BOB. I only want to do things I can do with you. Bob and Amelia, the best trash chefs, the best Polaroid photographers, the best rest stop lovemakers in America.

AMELIA. I wish I could just tear up all the roots of my life and stay with you but it's not that simple.

BOB. Forget about Chet. I hate Chet!

AMELIA. I've got to finish my list, Bob. I have one patch of time to accomplish something on my own and it might be the only chance I have. I can't give it up.

BOB. Let me help you with it! I know an on-duty policeman in Chicago —

AMELIA. This is a solo flight, Bob. Some great things aren't supposed to last forever. Like fruit.

BOB. We're more than a couple of fruits.

AMELIA. You've got your own list. And it is heartfelt and inspiring and overly ambitious. You need to pursue it. Forgive me.

BOB. I love you. *(Amelia kisses Bob. She gives Bob the Polaroid picture of their kiss. Bob finds a glass jar and gives it to Amelia.)* Don't give up on yourself, Amelia.

AMELIA. Keep looking for what you're looking for, Bob.

BOB. Promise me you won't go home when your list is checked.

AMELIA. Oh, Bob you know I have to —

BOB. Promise me you won't stop your journey and I won't stop mine. And then, maybe at some other rest stop somewhere, we can meet again.

AMELIA. Maybe we will.

BOB. You deserve happiness.

AMELIA. Good luck, Bob. *(Amelia runs off quickly.)*

BOB. YOU DESERVE HAPPINESS!

CHORUS TWO. It is said that Bob ran after Amelia's Lexus until she sped away, disappearing behind a school bus carrying a high school cheerleading squad to a regional competition. Amelia had already stayed too long with Bob to ever return to her past life, Bob's words echoing in her ear. And upon completing her final task, the filling of a jar with water from the Pacific Ocean, she began to think of the future. She thought of her namesake, of the great Amelia Earhart, and suddenly she felt fearless, and hopeful. She gathered driftwood, plastic and neck pillows scattered on the sand, laid on top of her newly made raft and began to drift west from the beach towards the islands of the South Pacific until she disappeared as her list, fully checked, broke apart in the water behind her. *(Bob holding the photograph.)*

BOB. This is where she kissed me. This is where she read me her list. This is where she never walked. This is where we … I hate this rest stop. I hate my shelter. I hate this table. I hate my books. "There's a journey ahead of you, Bob. Keep looking for what you're looking for." The great love of my life, Amelia not Earhart, said that.

CHORUS FOUR. And with that Bob took the only things of value that he had, put them into his underwear, and slipped into the trunk of a Ford Focus. *(Bob hops into a trunk.)*

BOB. Good luck, Bob.

End of Act Two

Interlude 2

A dance about love.

CHORUS TWO. This dance is about love. *(Chorus Two dances.)*
Thank you.

ACT THREE

ALL CHORUS. Bob. Act Three. *(Bob runs in with urinary urgency.)*
BOB. Clench clench clench.
CHORUS THREE. How Bob journeys across America, tries to do everything on his list, fails, meets an important man, and turns his back on everything he believes. *(Bob finds a bush. Pees.)*
BOB. Thank you, Caitlyn.
CHORUS FOUR. It is said the Ford Focus Bob jumped into drove for seven hours without stopping. Bob slept little, sweat a lot, and cried for various reasons he couldn't put into words.
BOB. *(A wordless noise.)* Ohhhhhhhhhh.
CHORUS TWO. It is said that the driver of the car was once again Jeanine's friend Bonnie who in the past seven years had attempted fresh starts with four different names: Barbara, Hillary, Laura and Michelle. *(Bonnie appears.)* Seeing Bob in her trunk once again, Bonnie was reminded how little had changed in her life and what was it, really, that she needed to feel comfortable in her own skin. *(Bonnie thinks very seriously about what she needs, exits.)*
CHORUS ONE. This is how Bob journeyed across America. *(Bob zips up and wanders into town.)*
BOB. Main Street. Maple Lane. Spruce Alley. Evergreen Boulevard. Deciduous Way. Washington, Madison, Franklin, Van Buren. The Mesquite Grill, El Sombrero, Luigi's, The Bamboo Wok. *(Darker incarnations of the road trip characters: A farmer walks by with a Monsanto-like seed bag, spirit crushed.)* Excuse me, hello there, farmer, can you tell me where I am? *(A delivery person walks by with a foreclosure notice or some other unwelcome delivery.)* Pardon me, delivery person, is there a good place to stay around here? *(A crazy person walks by.)* And ma'am, I recognize that you might be crazy, but can you tell me if this is a good place to live? *(An evil person walks by. Insert funny cultural icon of your choice here.)* Or ... Never mind. *(A diner table. Waitress One enters with a coffee mug and a pitcher.)*
WAITRESS ONE. New in town?
BOB. I am.
WAITRESS ONE. I can tell.
BOB. My clothes?

WAITRESS ONE. Just something wet about you.

BOB. I was in a car trunk so I might be a little damp —

WAITRESS ONE. Cream and sugar?

BOB. That's the only way I can drink it.

WAITRESS ONE. How sweet. *(Waitress Two brings in cream and sugar.)*

BOB. Could you tell me —

WAITRESS TWO. You want to hear the specials?

BOB. No. I'll have a ham and cheese omelet.

WAITRESS TWO. Oo, a man who knows what he wants.

BOB. My favorite breakfast. Been a long time since I've had a real one. *(Waitress Three brings in toast.)*

WAITRESS THREE. Bet you need some white toast too.

BOB. With extra butter.

WAITRESS THREE. Knew it in your eyes. *(Waitress Four brings in extra butter.)*

WAITRESS FOUR. So … what brings you to Sioux Falls?

BOB. Oh, is that where I —

WAITRESS ONE. And what brings you to Roanoke?

BOB. I thought I was in —

WAITRESS TWO. And to Aberdeen?

BOB. The birthplace of Kurt Cobain?

WAITRESS THREE. And South Padre Island?

WAITRESS ONE. Bloomington?

WAITRESS TWO. Glendive?

WAITRESS THREE. Montana?

WAITRESS FOUR. Lansing?

BOB. It's just where the trunk opened so I don't — *(The waitresses interrupt, overlapping.)*

WAITRESS ONE. Bella Vista?

WAITRESS TWO. Duluth?

WAITRESS THREE. Naples?

WAITRESS FOUR. Waterloo?

WAITRESS ONE. Middletown?

WAITRESS TWO. Portland?

WAITRESS THREE. Southampton?

WAITRESS FOUR. Las Cruces?

BOB. I've spent the last bunch of years thinking of ideas. Stuff I could do that might make a difference. And I wrote them down on a list. And now I'm looking for a place where I can do … things.

Solve problems. And maybe be recognized for it on a plaque or possibly a mountain.

WAITRESSES. Ohhhhhhh.

WAITRESS ONE. We got ourselves a dreamer.

WAITRESS TWO. Young blood.

WAITRESS THREE. Fresh meat.

WAITRESS FOUR. Your eyes haven't sunk into your skull yet.

BOB. Have you ever done anything great with your lives? *(The waitresses think.)*

WAITRESS ONE. I can be the only waitress in this diner, have it be packed and not miss a single order, not a single coffee mug dry.

WAITRESS TWO. I'm pretty good at quilts, how to tell a story and evoke memories through fabric. I gave one to my grandmother and it made her cry, so I consider that an accomplishment.

WAITRESS THREE. I'm the emperor of an online kingdom.

WAITRESS FOUR. I can tie a cherry stem into a knot with my tongue.

BOB. Maybe you can teach me.

WAITRESSES ONE, TWO and THREE. Maybe we can.

WAITRESS FOUR. It depends on your tongue. *(Each waitress puts a ham and cheese omelet in front of Bob.)*

BOB. Jeanine, who stole me, loved me and died, taught me that you could tell a lot about a place from the type of omelet that they make. Breakfast, unlike jazz, is America's gift to the world. Is this a place that honors that culinary legacy? Is it a place that would give someone a chance? *(Bob takes a bite of each omelet.)*

WAITRESS ONE. Is it?

BOB. I, uh, I think I'm going to go.

WAITRESSES. No!

BOB. Sorry, Those omelets are not very good.

WAITRESSES. No!

BOB. Something doesn't feel right about this place!

WAITRESSES. *(Various simultaneous muttering.)*

WAITRESS ONE. Well, yeah we know.

WAITRESS TWO. That's for sure.

WAITRESS THREE. Don't even get me started.

WAITRESS FOUR. That's 'cause we're situated on a hellmouth. *(The waitresses turn to Bob seductively.)*

WAITRESS ONE. We'd really love it if you stuck around for a score.

WAITRESS TWO. I could show you the new quilt cycle I'm working on.

WAITRESS THREE. And we really like having a fresh young face to look upon.

WAITRESS FOUR. I like the way your lips open and close.

BOB. You're all leaning so close to me.

WAITRESS ONE. You're exciting.

WAITRESS TWO. You have a mission.

WAITRESS THREE. Desire and passion.

WAITRESS FOUR. Is there anything we can do to convince you to stay? *(Sexy pause.)*

BOB. Maybe a bad omelet is an opportunity. There is a reason that trunk opened here and now. Because it is my job to transform this place from a drug-infested cesspool of decay into a Jacuzzi of opportunity and hope. And with this list I will — *(Waitress One kisses Bob.)*

WAITRESS ONE. Oh my.

BOB. That wasn't —

WAITRESS TWO. Bob.

BOB. I didn't mean to —

WAITRESS THREE. Bob Bob Bob.

BOB. I don't even remember telling you my name.

WAITRESS FOUR. You're a great kisser, Bob.

BOB. It could be my legacy. *(Beat. Bob kisses all of the waitresses. It becomes a group kiss and they fall to the ground. A bizarre lovemaking scene ensues.)*

WAITRESSES. Yes!

BOB. Yes.

WAITRESSES. Yes!

BOB. Yay.

WAITRESS ONE. You taste amazing, Bob! So fresh.

WAITRESS TWO. Like a lemon.

WAITRESS THREE. Fabric softener.

WAITRESS FOUR. Carbonation.

BOB. And you taste like peanut oil.

WAITRESSES. Mmmmm!

WAITRESS ONE. So passionate.

WAITRESS TWO. Hungry!

WAITRESS THREE. Strong!

WAITRESS FOUR. Moderately hairy.

BOB. So are you!

WAITRESS ONE. Let's get some of these clothes off, Bob.

BOB. Oh, that tickles.

WAITRESS TWO. Let's get these undies off, Bob.

BOB. Wait. There are some things in my undies that I need to —

WAITRESS THREE. I really want to get those undies off, Bob.

BOB. No, really, hold on, I keep stuff in there that I —

WAITRESS FOUR. Here I go, about to take off your undies!

BOB. NO! STOP! STOP STOP! *(Bob emerges from the sheet protecting his undies. The waitresses remain in a pile.)* I'm sorry.

WAITRESS ONE. I was on the cusp, Bob.

WAITRESS TWO. Your tenderness, Bob, you're really good at that.

WAITRESS THREE. Just feeling your weight, Bob, made me teeter.

WAITRESS FOUR. Where'd he go?

BOB. There are a lot of important things in my undies.

WAITRESS THREE. My petals were starting to open.

BOB. Lovemaking is only great with someone you love.

WAITRESS FOUR. *(Whispering to another waitress.)* I don't know if that's true.

BOB. Can I … just show you my list? *(A small waitress groan.)* Isn't it long? I've got a whole section on "ways to restore a dying town back to health." Tourism! We could work together. Some creative marketing and a fudge shoppe and —

WAITRESS ONE. Our husband's gonna be home soon.

BOB. You all have a husband.

WAITRESS TWO. He just doesn't scratch everything we need, you know.

BOB. Well then, find someone who can scratch it all.

WAITRESS THREE. We've got a pretty complicated itch, Bob.

BOB. "When you give up, you drown." The great escapist Harry Houdini said that. *(Beat.)*

WAITRESS FOUR. If you don't mind, let yourself out the back? Neighbors.

BOB. I don't think you realize how much tourists really love fudge.

WAITRESSES. Good luck, Bob.

WAITRESS ONE. And here's your change. *(Leaving a plastic change container with a dollar on it. Bob alone.)*

BOB. *(Reading the dollar.)* "Barry Metcalf is still a slut." And what am I? *(Bob journeys across America.)*

CHORUS TWO. Three hundred seventeen towns. Twenty-three unopened fudge shops. Eleven hundred waitresses. And Bob was unable to accomplish anything on his list.

BOB. *(Crossing each item off his list.)* Nobody will give me a chance.

CHORUS ONE. Bob was reduced to performing some of the worst jobs in the nation. *(A chain coffee shop.)*

BOB. Ventino Quadruple low-fat-half-caf mocha latte for Deborah.

CHORUS THREE. But, much like a Cubs fan, Bob would enter each new chapter with a small amount of hope. *(Bob hands the drink to the customer, grabs her arm.)*

BOB. This could be better than it is, Deborah. If they let me make it how it should be made, with a little pitcher for the milk and grace in the pour, it could change your life.

CHORUS THREE. And much like a Cubs fan, Bob's hope would quickly fade.

BARISTA. Customers do not need to be made aware of the mediocrity.

BOB. This is an opportunity to affect another person on this planet.

BARISTA. You're a barista.

DEBORAH. My arm.

BOB. There are great baristas out there.

BARISTA. I majored in literature. At Cornell.

BOB. They have barista competitions and their own dirty style!

BARISTA. I was going to be the cultural critic of *The New Yorker*.

BOB. That's amazing!

BARISTA. It would have been, if I was the cultural critic of *The New Yorker*! If life were actually fair, if the UPenn mafia didn't control the publishing world, if Sybil hadn't called me promiscuous on every dollar she had … my dream is over, dude.

DEBORAH. Let go of my arm.

BOB. Start your own magazine. Host culture at the store. Make it a critical Mecca.

BARISTA. Dude dude dude, chill the 'bition. Don't you see what Deborah and I are doing? The whole suffering of life gets a little bit lighter when you just give up. *(Bob punches barista.)* Why did you do that?

BOB. BECAUSE WE ARE ALL GOING TO DIE OR DISAPPEAR. Vanish into small little bits and break hearts. And before that happens, before it all gets taken away, I'm supposed to be great at something. Even if it's foam.

BARISTA. You just punched me.

BOB. I am Bob and I will be a great man.

BARISTA. You're delusional, Bob.

BOB. You're a slut, Barry Metcalf.

BARISTA. You're fired, Bob.

BOB. I fire you! *(Barista punches Bob.)* You are all fools! *(Barista punches Bob.)* YOU ARE DOOMING THIS NATION TO SMALL DREAMS. *(Deborah punches Bob.)*

BARISTA. You're the dream. *(Punches Bob, he falls to the ground.)* I'm reality. Get it, dude?

DEBORAH. Don't make me feel bad for what I've settled for. *(Deborah kicks Bob.)*

BARISTA. Now get the hell out of Poncha Springs! *(Barista and Deborah walk off arm in arm on their way to have sex. Bob crawls into the boxcar of a freight train, wipes his bloody face.)*

BOB. Create catharsis through artistically moving beverages. *(Crosses it off his list.)* What degrading act will I be forced to perform next? I don't know what to do anymore.

GUNTHER. Sounds like you haven't found your Ringer Traum Yet. *(A match is struck and a lantern lit revealing Gunther [Chorus Four], a roughly dressed man who looks like he may have been strikingly handsome back in the day but now has some wreckage.)*

BOB. Sorry, I didn't realize this boxcar was taken.

GUNTHER. Trade you a drink for some food.

BOB. All I have are muffin wrappers.

GUNTHER. My favorite. *(Bob gives Gunther a couple muffin wrappers. Gunther takes a swig and passes flask to Bob. Gunther chews.)* Blueberry?

BOB. Reduced-Fat blueberry bran.

GUNTHER. Pretty good buds you got.

BOB. I used to sell them. Took the wrappers out of the trash. *(Bob takes a sip and coughs.)* What is this?

GUNTHER. It's whin.

BOB. Never heard of it.

GUNTHER. My own special blend of whiskey and gin. Bottom shelf.

BOB. Oh.

GUNTHER. I only have one flask.

BOB. It's awful.

GUNTHER. Give it a few years and it goes down smooth. *(Bob gives back the flask.)* Something gnawing on your bone, tiger?

BOB. It's my birthday.

GUNTHER. On Valentine's Day? How sweet.

BOB. I'm thirty years old.

GUNTHER. Young buck.

BOB. Before they turned thirty, Bill Gates founded Microsoft, Carolyn Davidson designed the Nike swoosh, and Jimi Hendrix already died. My greatest achievement to date is survival.

GUNTHER. Don't knock survival. Not easy keeping the blood pumping, hoping the wolves don't get you along the way.

BOB. I need to be more than alive. *(Beat.)*

GUNTHER. I used to be more than alive.

BOB. Yeah, I'm sure you were.

GUNTHER. Perhaps you would be illuminated by my life story.

BOB. Actually I was thinking I might close my —

GUNTHER. My name is Gunther Roy.

BOB. Hi. I'm —

GUNTHER. I used to be known as the greatest animal trainer of all time. Lions, tigers, llamas, anything with a compound eye.

BOB. Sorry, I've never heard of —

GUNTHER. I toured for thirty years with the largest circus in the country. I stuck my head into the mouth of a lion. I made tigers jump through flaming hoops. I made geese fly in formations that spelled letters of the alphabet. USA.

BOB. That sounds pretty —

GUNTHER. My closing act was called the "CreatureMaker" where I would command a lion and a tiger to mate. No other trainer could do that. But then one night changed everything. Do you want to hear about the night that changed everything?

BOB. Maybe in an hour, I'm tired and still bleeding and I —

GUNTHER. This is Gunther's flashback!

BOB. OK. *(At the circus. Helen runs in.)*

HELEN. Mr. Roy, that was amazing!

GUNTHER. Why thank you, little fawn.

HELEN. A lion and a tiger! And they seemed to enjoy it!

GUNTHER. They don't.

HELEN. I'm an animal trainer too.

GUNTHER. Oh. How wonderful.

HELEN. Aspiring. I work at a pet store to pay the bills.

GUNTHER. What have you forced animals to do so far?

HELEN. Little stuff. Getting sheep into various shapes: pentagons, rhombuses and whatnot. Got a whole coop of chickens to play dead when I rang a gong. That sort of thing.

GUNTHER. Pretty impressive. For a lady.

HELEN. Helen. My name is Helen.

CHORUS ONE and TWO. *(Whisper.)* Helen.

BOB. Helen …

GUNTHER. You smell like celery, Helen.

HELEN. Animals have been more faithful and loving to me than any person. And training is my life.

GUNTHER. What is your RingerTraum, Helen?

HELEN. You want to know my RingerTraum?

BOB. What is a … wait, how do you even say —

GUNTHER. Every great animal trainer has a RingerTraum. The dream they have, standing in the center ring, performing the one seemingly impossible act they've dedicated their entire life to being able to achieve.

BOB. I need one of those. 'Cause I have this big list and it is not —

GUNTHER. *(To Bob.)* Quiet!

HELEN. I've never told anyone.

GUNTHER. It's the most important thing to know about you. What is Helen's RingerTraum?

HELEN. I call it the "Living Totem." A tribute to nature and our Native American ancestors. A prairie dog sitting on top of a bald eagle perched on top of a beaver lying on a wolf standing on a mountain lion hunched on a grizzly bear that's got each paw on one of four buffalo. After they stack up, the lights would dim, and I would ask the audience … "What animal are you? Which one is your guide on the trail of life? You are not alone." I want my act to cause inspiration, revelation and tears.

GUNTHER and BOB. *(Gunther threatened.)* That is the most impressive RingerTraum I have ever heard.

HELEN. That's nice of you to say.

GUNTHER. Helen, you have the potential to become the greatest animal trainer of all time.

HELEN. You don't really mean that.

GUNTHER. Unless someone can stop you.

HELEN. If I can't become a trainer, my life will be nothing but misery.

GUNTHER. Well then, you should join the circus, Helen.

BOB. Yes, she should.

HELEN. Right now?

GUNTHER. You can be my assistant.

HELEN. You're joking.

GUNTHER. I can keep an eye on you.

HELEN. I was just hoping for an autograph and a photo.

GUNTHER. Is that a yes?

HELEN. Yes yes!

BOB. Yes!

GUNTHER. Then we must kiss!

HELEN. Mr. Roy?

GUNTHER. To be a great trainer and assistant team, the animals must sense that we are mates, that we have tasted of each other, our smells intertwined, that we would defend each other's life with brutal conviction.

HELEN. Can't we just rub handkerchiefs on each other?

GUNTHER. Animals could smell that lie. Join me, Helen. Sow your talent. Kiss my lips.

HELEN. You better not be just saying things to seduce me.

GUNTHER. Are you scared, Helen?

HELEN. I am never scared, Mr. Roy. Even if it kills me, I will do whatever it takes to be the greatest trainer that I can.

GUNTHER. Tonight, we begin the great collaboration of Helen and Gunther Roy.

HELEN. Helen and Gunther Roy.

GUNTHER. Who knows what we can create together? *(Back to the freight train.)*

BOB. I bet you created something amazing.

GUNTHER. It was the most incredible night of hanky panky I've ever known. Heaven and earth crashing together, lightning striking water, making life.

BOB. That's the best kind.

GUNTHER. Well, Gunther Roy, for the first time, got scared.

BOB. But you conquered your fears and together you were the greatest animal act team the world has ever seen!

GUNTHER. When Helen ran home to pack her toiletries and leotards, I told the circus that something happened between a child and a clown, and we quickly left town. I had Helen blacklisted from all the other circuses, the animal schools, zoos ... I made sure she would never train again. *(Helen runs in with a packed bag. Looks around at an empty lot, spinning.)*

BOB. No. No no no.

GUNTHER. When she described the RingerTraum she had, I knew she would unseat my title as the Greatest Animal Trainer of All Time. And so, much like a baby elephant, her spirit had to be crushed.

BOB. That's … terrible!

GUNTHER. Of course it is.

BOB. You destroyed her dream.

GUNTHER. Forty weeks later a voicemail was left on my trailer phone. *(Helen appears, post-birth, a phone booth outside the White Castle.)*

HELEN. Dear Mr. Roy. I should have known by the way you whip goats how cruel you really are. Now I know. You have bound another soul, cue the music. I thought you should know that your act has resulted in a baby boy. He's got your frown. Something sparkly about him but one sight of his face makes me want to rob his clothes. And so I have left him in a White Castle to fend for himself. Somewhere in America, your firstborn son is living. If you want to go find him and tell him things are different than you've shown them to me to be, be my guest. Until you do, I curse you to live a life that befits the type of trainer that you are. *(A distant lion's roar.)* Good luck. *(Helen runs off, crying.)*

BOB. You deserved that voicemail.

GUNTHER. The animals sensed it immediately. They began to lose their fear and one day, when I stuck my face into the mouth of Mary Jo Sabre, I felt her jaw close just enough that I couldn't remove my head. I think she would have closed all the way if I hadn't shot her in the head with my gun. And from that moment I have lived a curs-ed life, of sadness and suffering that not even a full jug of whin can obscure.

BOB. You had the opportunity to create something amazing. And you didn't. You're not a great man at all!

GUNTHER. All I wish is to redeem my existence just a little. And so I tirelessly wander across this land, looking for that boy that's got a bit of me placed in him thirty years ago. *(Beat.)*

BOB. Thirty years ago.

GUNTHER. Yeah. Thirty years and nine months. *(Beat.)*

BOB. I'm thirty years old.

GUNTHER. Happy birthday.

BOB. I was born in a White Castle.

GUNTHER. I've heard worse.

BOB. I've never met my birth parents.

GUNTHER. I'm searching for my boy.

BOB. I'm not a girl. *(Beat.)*

GUNTHER. Smile. *(Bob smiles.)* That's her smile.

BOB. Frown. *(Gunther frowns.)* I've got your frown.

GUNTHER. I thought it looked familiar.

BOB. Father?

GUNTHER. Son.

BOB. Out of all the boxcars on this train.

GUNTHER. What's your name, son?

BOB. Bob.

GUNTHER. That's a short name.

BOB. Until this moment, my history started on a floor. But now I know why. And it's a wild, awful, passionate reason.

GUNTHER. Can you forgive me?

BOB. Teach me to tame lions.

GUNTHER. Oh boy.

BOB. Teach me to be fearless in the face of peril. Teach me to perform incredible acts that make an audience cheer.

GUNTHER. I don't think I know how to do that anymore.

BOB. I could be your assistant. We can get some new animals, find a small circus. I could help you drink whin at a more moderate level.

GUNTHER. Oh, that sounds so scary. I'm so scared, Bob!

BOB. I am your son. Show me things are different than you showed them to Helen to be. And your curse will be lifted. Be the trainer that you are. *(Beat.)*

GUNTHER. You have any pets?

BOB. Just some fleas.

GUNTHER. That's a start. *(They hug.)* Now the first thing you need to know is — *(The sound of hungry and vicious wolves.)*

BOB. What is that?

GUNTHER. That is the sound of hungry and vicious wolves.

BOB. Oh no. We must have entered the Nevada desert freight train yard!

GUNTHER. There! *(A pack of wolves appear.)*

BOB. So many of them!

GUNTHER. Thirsty for blood.

BOB. The train is slowing down!

GUNTHER. If they don't eat us first, the railroad guards will.

BOB. Don't be scared, Dad. We're together! We can fight 'em off. Father and son!

44

GUNTHER. Wolves can't be fought.

BOB. Then we will run into the desert as fast we can!

GUNTHER. I CAN'T RUN WITH THESE KNEES! *(Gunther makes a decision.)* Oh, Bob —

BOB. Oh, no.

GUNTHER. I wish I could share with you all sorts of animal training lessons, my favorite hobo recipes, or how to survive in a desert.

BOB. Don't talk like this.

GUNTHER. If you need to, you can drink your own pee.

BOB. I don't like it when people give me urgent final lessons.

GUNTHER. It's looking like my only gift to you is saving your life.

BOB. I want to hang out with you. Live in a trailer, cook omelets together and laugh about sad things. You were about to tell me the first thing I need to —

GUNTHER. THIS IS MY RINGERTRAUM, BOB! FIND YOUR OWN!

BOB. But I don't know how!

GUNTHER. Good luck, Bob. JUMP! *(They jump off the freight car.)*

BOB. AHHH!

GUNTHER. *(Running towards wolves.)* AHHHH! *(The wolves eat Gunther. Probably offstage. Gunther's arm flies in. An angry prayer.)*

BOB. Are you listening, Barry Metcalf? Are you listening, Poncha Springs? I have a father, who lived hard, smelled rough, who has done some terrible things in his life and he's still a greater man than all of you! And somewhere in America I have a mother who has the power to curse through voicemails. Who had a beautiful RingerTraum. And I have her smile. And they've ruined their lives for me. You evil, selfish, despicable land. You eat my father, poison my Jeanine, steal my Amelia, and you have soiled every beautiful idea I've written on pieces of paper with your mediocre filth. You are killing everything I love! Well, I curse you, Barry Metcalf. I curse Sioux Falls, Roanoke, and Aberdeen. I curse this ENTIRE NATION to live a life that befits who they are! No more fudge shops. No more lists. America does not deserve the love and passion of a dreamer. But I do. I have a dream. And I will pursue it by any means necessary until there is justice, until the pain you have inflicted upon me is avenged. I have a RINGERTRAUM and BOB WILL NOT BE STOPPED. Good luck, Bob. Good luck, indeed. *(He walks. Blackout. Intermission.)*

End of Act Three

Interlude Three

A dance about luck.

CHORUS FOUR. This is a dance about luck. *(Chorus Four does the dance.)* Thank you.

ACT FOUR

ALL CHORUS. Bob. Act Four.

CHORUS FOUR. How Bob has a turn of luck, becomes a new man, achieves a false dream, meets an important woman and is redeemed.

CHORUS THREE. This is how Bob had a turn of luck. *(A doorbell rings in a very large house. Tony, a butler, heads for the door.)*

BOB. No! *(Bob, 50 years old, perhaps dressed like Hugh Hefner [fancy pajamas], enters. He holds two glasses of champagne.)* I'll get it, Tony!

TONY. Yes, Bob. *(Tony exits. Bob opens the door.)*

BOB. Just in time! The Jacuzzi is at the perfect temperature for — Oh.

VERA. Hello!

BOB. You are not who I was expecting.

VERA. My name is Vera Ponchatraine and I am a member of Troop 599: The greatest scouting troop of any gender in the Nevada area!

BOB. What do you want?

VERA. Did you know that there are over 1.3 million homeless and abandoned youths in the United States?

BOB. Oh no.

VERA. Yes, it is sad. All of us in Troop 599 are blessed to come from loving families, except for Bernadette Winters, and we would like to share a small portion of our blessings with those who are cursed. So, our troop is building a brand-new shelter for abandoned children in the Nevada desert area. Because everyone deserves a place they will not feel alone. Would you be interested in purchasing a box of cookies to support our cause?

BOB. Would I be interested?

VERA. If I sell the most cookies, I win tickets to Water Kingdom. *(Beat. Bob laughs. Not so nicely.)* What's so funny?

BOB. I used to be like you. "Doing Good Deeds." "Save The World." "Thin Mints." Guess where that got me?

VERA. It looks like you're doing very —

BOB. It seems like only twenty minutes ago that I was in the middle of the desert, no food or water, everything I loved robbed from me except for a ring in my undies moist with scrotal dew. For all practical purposes I should be dead. You know what death is, little girl?

VERA. Yes, my brother —

BOB. The point is, I'm not dead. I'm here living richly in this huge house. Isn't my house amazing?

VERA. It's very large.

BOB. And my silk pajamas. Don't they look comfy?

VERA. They're kind of opening up at the —

BOB. How do you think I did it, Brownie?

VERA. Did you pray?

BOB. No, *chica*, I got my feet under myself, cursed the nation, picked a direction, and I walked. *(Bob's flashback/story begins.)* Across hot sand. Past nuclear testing sites, foreclosed homes, and a terrible "arts" festival that was lighting something stupid on fire. I hunted and ate beetles, threw sand at vultures that were bird-kissing my flanks with their sharp, hungry beaks, and I followed the only piece of advice my recently met and killed birth father gave me and drank my own pee.

VERA. There's a lot of ammonia in —

BOB. And I kept yelling at myself, "Don't die, Bob! Keep crawling, Bob, and prove Poncha Springs wrong!"

VERA. Who?

BOB. I crawled for forty days and nights or thereabouts until one scorching day that hot sand became grass, and that grass became a fountain and that fountain had a pathway that led to the floor of this very building.

VERA. You just crawled into your house?

BOB. The Martin Luther Casino. The only civil rights-themed casino and adult playground in the country. "Martin Luther Casino: What's Your Dream?" That was the message blinking above the door.

VERA. That sounds wrong

BOB. But I had a dream. And, much like the creators of the greatest musical ever, *Mamma Mia*, I knew I had to risk everything I had. *(A roulette wheel spins in a melancholy way. A one armed roulette dealer stands by the wheel. Bob staggers towards it. There are two onlookers.)*

DEALER. Roulette wheel. Ye tired, ye poor, ye huddled. Come to my wheel and place your bets.

BOB. It's so beautiful.

DEALER. You look like Walt Whitman.

BOB. It's a sign.

DEALER. It's a wheel.

BOB. I want justice. I want a different life. Can I do that here?

DEALER. Depends on what you risk. The more it hurts, the bigger the win. *(Showing stump.)* What you gonna bet? *(Bob pulls out the ring.)*

BOB. Everything I have.

DEALER. What a moist ring.

VERA. You shouldn't bet that. You should be saving that for someone special.

BOB. Saving it for me. Roulette dealer, if I win, I promise I will honor and avenge the deaths of all I have loved. I will never again be slave to fools. I promise I will not be the man I used to be.

DEALER. Deal.

BOB. Red. Red is blood. I bet this ring on red.

DEALER. No more bets at this table please, this gentleman has bet it all. What do the Fates have in store for us tonight? A story of joy or a story to learn from? It all depends on this one little shiny ...

BALL! *(Sound of the ball rolling, bouncing and landing in a slot. Putting down the marker.)* 30. Red. *(Vera stifles a clap.)*

BOB. Yes!

VERA. Yes!

BOB. This is my moment.

VERA. Yeah, that's, oo ... Well done.

BOB. Double or nothing!

VERA. No!

BOB. And if I lose, kill me. On the casino floor. Drag me through the streets, place my head on a spire along I-15.

VERA. My brother doubled or nothing'd and they found him —

BOB. This is my flashback, Sashy! Red again!

DEALER. BALL! *(Sound of the ball rolling, bouncing and landing in a slot.)* Twenty-seven. Red.

VERA. Amazing! Oh wow! That's amazing! Holy cow.

BOB. It's not enough.

DEALER and VERA. Enough for what?

BOB. Again!

DEALER. Red.

BOB. Again!

DEALER. Red.

BOB. Again! Again! Again!

VERA. My tummy hurts.

BOB. And I won again. And again and again and again and that wheel landed on red seventeen times! *(The flashback fades out.)*

VERA. A hundred and thirty-one thousand times the value of the ring.

BOB. And I would have kept going if the Martin Luther Casino hadn't gone bankrupt and everyone lost their jobs and they had to turn their property over to me and is now my very home in which you solicit in today.

VERA. Wow, sir, it sounds like you were very, very lucky.

BOB. THERE IS NO SUCH THING AS LUCK! When Rockefeller was born at the right place at the right time, he monopolized. When Judy Garland chanced the part of Dorothy, she knocked it out of the park. And when Lou Gehrig stumbled upon a new disease, he made sure his name would last forever. I risked my life for this. I crawled towards a window and I jumped. Don't tell me that's not work, girlfriend.

VERA. I don't want to be your girlfriend.

BOB. Tell your little homeless children buddies that maybe they should stop hoping for handouts from ugly girls who really just want free tickets to Water Kingdom.

VERA. It's true what they say about you.

BOB. What do they say about me?

VERA. That you are not a very nice man.

BOB. No. No, I am not a nice man. Nothing great ever happens from being nice.

VERA. I told my pastor I was going to save you.

BOB. The only reason I answered the door is that I thought you were a prostitute!

VERA. Mom! *(Vera runs off.)*

BOB. Yeah, run back to Mommy! Run back to the parent who's alive and loves you! Hug her tight, mommyhaver! *(Door slams. Bob alone.)*

CHORUS. *(Whisper.)* Bob. *(Bob looks around. Whisper.)* Bob. *(Bob looks around.)*

BOB. Quiet.

CHORUS. *(Whisper.)* Not a nice man, Bob.

BOB. Music! *(Music plays.)*

CHORUS THREE. It is said that in the twenty years since Bob had his "this is not luck I totally earned this" moment, Bob had become the three thousand two hundred and seventh richest person in America.

BOB. Champagne! *(Tony brings Bob a glass of champagne.)*

CHORUS FOUR. Bob bought new clothes, got a butler, and put his money into Goldman Sachs instead of pillowcases where he made tons of money gambling on the misfortune of others.

BOB. Cake! *(Tony enters with birthday cake.)*

CHORUS ONE. Bob's kisses tasted different, he drank espresso from a can and he would occasionally lock himself in hotel rooms and urinate in jars. Bob never left the casino grounds and his eyes, the ones that saved him, had sunk into his skull.

TONY. Happy fiftieth birthday, Bob.

BOB. She knew about me.

TONY. Who, Bob?

BOB. Apparently I have a reputation in the female scouting community for "not being nice."

TONY. You must feel proud, Bob.

BOB. The world that you live in is not nice, Vera!

TONY. I don't think she can hear you, Bob. *(Bob pees in a jar.)*

BOB. I have everything I need. Money. A casino turned into a house. A butler.

TONY. That is the trifecta, Bob.

BOB. I don't need validation from "Scouts." I don't need a "birthday party" with "guests." I think I'm going to lock myself in room seven-oh-nine.

TONY. Bob …

BOB. Please no lesson on my birthday, Tony.

TONY. Bob, I have been a butler for several hundred years as I possess both a tremendous ability to attend to people's whims and a rare genetic disease where I shall never age nor die. I've seen money transform some of the most decent people. My last employer, a successful and mediocre entertainer, insisted I put diamonds in her salad. She wanted to feel them pass through her abdomen, come out the back, after which she planned to sell them on her website. She would have done so if the diamonds had not sliced through her small intestine, bleeding her dead in less than two hours.

BOB. Are you saying it was wrong to pursue my happiness?

51

TONY. Are you happy, Bob?

BOB. What makes you think I'm not happy?

TONY. You seem a little lonely, Bob.

BOB. You seem a little lonely, Tony.

TONY. You could be a great man, Bob.

BOB. I am a great man.

TONY. Prove it.

BOB. You prove it.

TONY. I asked first.

BOB. Let me eat cake.

TONY. Happy birthday, Bob. *(Tony exits.)*

BOB. Nobody knows what I've been through. Nobody understands who I am.

CHORUS ONE. *(As Vera. Whisper.)* You are not a nice man, Bob.

BOB. Quiet.

CHORUS. *(Whisper.)* You're not a nice man, Bob.

BOB. Shhh! *(The Chorus, haunting.)*

CHORUS ONE. D minus again, Bob.

CHORUS TWO. Bob, the way you play hockey, I don't know what to feel.

CHORUS THREE. I don't want to stay over at Bob's.

CHORUS FOUR. You were just awkward at recess, Bob.

BOB. Let me eat cake!

CHORUS ONE. You're not even a historian, Bob.

CHORUS TWO. You're a terrible artist, Bob.

CHORUS THREE. Don't cure, Bob. Don't cure the sick.

CHORUS FOUR. Bob, you can't lead us.

BOB. I could if I wanted. *(Chorus, as past characters.)*

CHORUS ONE. I raised you in my Malibu to be better than this, Bob.

CHORUS TWO. I thought you'd use my ring for goodness, Bob.

CHORUS THREE. You are not the man that I kissed, Bob.

CHORUS FOUR. You are not a trainer's son, Bob.

BOB. Yes I am!

CHORUS ONE. Who are you, Bob?

CHORUS TWO and THREE. Who are you, Bob?

CHORUS FOUR. Bob has been stopped.

BOB. No, no, I have not been stopped! Maybe it's time I did prove it to you, Tony. Vera. I am capable of great things. I will create something amazing. Something that will take away breath. Something really really large. It's time to show this nation who Bob really is. *(Bob runs off.)*

CHORUS FOUR. It is said that Bob ran into the scene shop of the abandoned French-Canadian civil rights cirque show, *Egalité,* and ordered thousands of products from the Home Depot. For years Bob worked every day, and Tony heard noises from various machines, materials, yells of triumph —

BOB. *[A yell of triumph.]*

CHORUS FOUR. Yells of despair.

BOB. *[A curse of despair.]*

CHORUS FOUR. And yells of ambiguity.

BOB. *[An ambiguous yell.]*

CHORUS FOUR. And then on Bob's fifty-fifth birthday —

BOB. *(Singing.)* It is finished!

CHORUS TWO. Under cover of night and a sheet, Bob packed his creation into an oversize trailer attached to an RV, and hired three prostitutes to join him and Tony on a road trip. In the Black Hills of South Dakota, Bob pulled off Interstate 90 and drove towards a national monument that was dear to his heart. However, Bob's vehicle was too large for the windy mountain road to make it all the way.

BOB. *(Off.)* Shoot! Fine.

CHORUS THREE. And so Bob was forced to pull into an overflow parking lot eight miles away from the Mount Rushmore Visitor Center, where he pulled out his creation from his trailer, covered by a sheet where it sat in a large vehicle parking spot. This is how Bob achieved a false dream. *(Bob stands next to a sheet covering something. Tony and three prostitutes are also there, a little bewildered.)*

BOB. This way, Tony, prostitutes. You are a witness to one of the greatest achievements ever performed by a single person in America. A testament to what one man can do by himself, if they are someone like me.

PROSTITUTE THREE. Is it a death ray?

PROSTITUTE FOUR. A time machine.

PROSTITUTE ONE. A portal to another dimension.

BOB. All those things and more, my hired friends.

TONY. Oh, Bob, this is so exciting. I am so excited right now.

BOB. Eight miles from this very spot a fire was lit inside my soul and started a lifelong dream. We all have big dreams of what we hope to achieve in this world, and most of us are too stupid or lazy to achieve it. But I am not. I am someone whose dream has come true. *(Bob rips off an unseen sheet. Everyone looks up.)*

PROSTITUTE ONE. What is it?

BOB. It's my face. Chiseled in granite. And if you stand over here, and if I blow up that big chunk of mountain in between, it's as though I'm next to Abe Lincoln himself. And the best part, underneath …

PROSTITUTE THREE. Ohh. It's a plaque in a boulder.

PROSTITUTE FOUR. A mountain with your face on it.

PROSTITUTE ONE. And a plaque.

TONY. Oh, Bob.

BOB. I had to make it over fifty times to get it right. The bronze letters, the leathery background … And this boulder looks like it could last for millions of years. *(He rubs his fingers across the plaque.)* I like the sound that it makes when I rub my fingers across my name. Did you hear that? *(He rubs it again.)* I can almost see my reflection in the letters. I see me in me. That's funny. Hello me. *(He kisses the plaque.)*

PROSTITUTE ONE. Did you say there was cheese?

BOB. I hope a child eats lunch on this. And she'll wonder who she's sitting on. And for a moment, I will exist again under her shorts. And she'll wonder if one day, she could be me.

PROSTITUTE THREE. *(Half-hearted.)* Yay. She could be you! *(Bad clapping.)*

BOB. So? What do you think, Tony? Whores?

TONY. Oh, Bob.

PROSTITUTE FOUR. Is it wine time?

BOB. This is everything I've always wanted.

TONY. It's a very good plaque, Bob.

PROSTITUTE ONE. Yeah, let's celebrate.

PROSTITUTE FOUR. Celebrate. *(!)*

PROSTITUTE THREE. How about we go to the RV and —

BOB. I AM BOB AND I AM A GREAT MAN AND I AM ON A PLAQUE! *(They stare at him.)* IS THIS NOT ENOUGH FOR YOU?

PROSTITUTE ONE. Yes.

PROSTITUTE FOUR. No?

PROSTITUTE THREE. I don't think I understand the —

BOB. Leave me alone. *(The prostitutes leave.)*

TONY. Bob.

BOB. You're fired, Tony!

TONY. I fire you. *(The sound of an RV driving away. Bob, alone by his plaque.)*

BOB. That didn't go how I thought it would. Bob, would you pack your child into a car, drive thousands of miles to show her this plaque? I'm sorry, Jeanine. Amelia, Gunther, Connor, James the Bear … I'm sorry you believed in me. *(Bob breaks down. A long beat. It begins to snow. Days pass. Sven, a wolf, enters.)* And here comes the wolf. Can you smell my weakness and failure? Have you come all the way from the freight train yard to find your next snack? Well, here I am. Take me. Thin out the human herd. Sink your teeth into my flesh and don't stop chomping till you get to my heart. *(Sven licks Bob's nose.)* Hey. *(Sven starts licking Bob's face. Unseen, Helen enters, wearing the pants she stole from Bob in Act One.)* Hey, stop it!

HELEN. He's a licker.

BOB. What?

HELEN. Loves salt. You must have a lot on your skin.

BOB. He's tickling me. Hey!

HELEN. Sven! Off! *(Sven stops licking, stares at Bob.)* His tongue can be relentless.

BOB. I was hoping he'd put me out of my misery.

HELEN. He's only done that a couple times. Wanna see a trick?

BOB. I'm not really in the mood for —

HELEN. Sven! *(Sven gets alert.)* Do Fosse. *(Sven does a small four-legged Bob Fosse-esque dance.)*

BOB. That's pretty good.

HELEN. I'm teaching Sven to dance in all the great choreographer styles. You should see his Cunningham.

BOB. I like that trick.

HELEN. I call it "Helen and the Dancing Wolf."

OTHER CHORUS. Helen. *(Bob hears the whisper.)*

HELEN. I need to gloss up the act a bit. Maybe sequins. That was the feedback we got at our Vegas audition. In a few years, if I'm lucky, I'll have a whole menagerie of creatures and you won't believe what I'd like 'em to do. Shuffle off now, Sven. *(Sven shuffles off.)*

BOB. He seems nice.

HELEN. Poor thing has so many fleas, can't ever get rid of 'em. But the dancing makes him forget. You got any?

BOB. Fleas?

HELEN. I bet you're pretty great with animals.

BOB. I'm not great with anything.

HELEN. But it's in your blood, Bob.

OTHER CHORUS. *(Whisper.)* Bob. *(Beat.)*

BOB. Something about your face.

HELEN. I don't think you'd remember my — *(Bob sees Helen's pants.)*

BOB. Oh my goodness. You … you —

HELEN. That's right, Bob —

BOB. *(Simultaneous with Helen.)* YOU STOLE MY PANTS. *(Beat.)* Wait. No. You're my mother?	HELEN. *(Simultaneous with Bob.)* I AM YOUR MOTHER. Whoa. Really? I stole your pants?

BOB. I don't believe it.

HELEN. How godawful is that?

BOB. Helen.

HELEN. Bob.

BOB. How did you find me?

HELEN. Well, you look like half of him and half of me.

BOB. Yeah, but —

HELEN. And then Sven licked you. Only does that to kin.

BOB. What do you want from me?

HELEN. I don't want anything from you.

BOB. Come out of the woodwork to collect on the good fortune of your long-lost son.

HELEN. I want to help you.

BOB. I'm doing fine. I have this glorious monument constructed in my honor, which is amazing, and you are disturbing my celebration.

HELEN. Oh sweetie, hollow plaques never made anyone happy.

BOB. Well, I am happy. Here's a hundred dollars for some sequins. I hope everything works out wonderfully for you and Sven and I hope you get all the animals you need for your Living Totem.

HELEN. You know about that?

BOB. It's amazing and beautiful. Now goodbye. And good luck! *(Helen starts to walk off. Stops.)*

HELEN. I'm sorry.

BOB. For dumping me in a bathroom?

HELEN. No, that was for the best. Stealing your pants, now that's just cruel.

BOB. They were my favorite pants.

HELEN. That day was my lowest after a terrible string of lows.

My parents died in a mining explosion, had my life-dream destroyed, a baby I hated and dumped, lost my drive, my confidence, my job, my home, some teeth, and got taken advantage of by a credit card company. Ever had a rough go like that?

BOB. Something like it.

HELEN. Things had gotten so desperate for me I had resorted to robbing clothes from children just to get by. But that day, you, I can't believe it was you, something in the way you walked, the embarrassment of being in the middle of the street in your BVDs was the least of your worries ... I knew I had just stolen from someone who had no home to run to.

BOB. But you did it anyway.

HELEN. Stealing from you devastated me. I was on my way to throwing myself into the lake when I walked by the Art Institute, and I saw this cop on the steps, crying ferociously.

BOB. I know that cop.

HELEN. I watched him put his palms all over the steps and then lick his hands.

BOB. I know what he was licking.

HELEN. And I thought, oh, there is someone else in the world with as much pain and regret as me. Something made me want to talk to him. He told me the story of the great mistake he made in his life. And I told him mine.

BOB. So many great mistakes.

HELEN. We got married. Almost forty years. We were pretty happy. Connor passed away a few years ago. Shot in the liver by a deep-dish pizza maker.

BOB. He was a good man. He gave me this ring.

HELEN. As he filled with liquid in all the wrong places, we reminisced about how we met that day at the museum steps. He told me about the boy who told him where his first love was. "How sad for a son so young," I said, "to have their mother die in his arms." *(Connor appears.)*

CONNOR. It wasn't her son.

HELEN. Who was he?

CONNOR. It was a boy she'd found as a baby in a White Castle on Valentine's Day. *(Jeanine appears.)*

HELEN. My baby!

CONNOR. He said he had to be a great man for her. His name was ...

CONNOR and BOB. ... Bob. *(Connor dies. He and Jeanine disappear.)*

HELEN. And are you a "great man," Bob?

BOB. I'm smart, I'm well-meaning, and I'm pretty good at making love.

HELEN. All good things.

BOB. But if I never existed, would anything be different?

HELEN. That's an unanswerable question, Bob.

BOB. I wanted to have an answer. I guess sometimes we're not who we hope we are.

HELEN. Ain't that the truth. *(Beat.)*

BOB. So what is the point of even trying?

HELEN. Well, Bob, I'm here to tell you —

BOB. What is the purpose of moving forward when you know you'll fail?

HELEN. You don't know that, that's not the —

BOB. Why even live another day, breathe another breath on this planet when you — *(Helen slaps Bob.)* Ow!

HELEN. Why do you want to spend precious breaths of life on this little pity party you got going on here?

BOB. But I —

HELEN. Doesn't do anyone a lick of good!

BOB. But —

HELEN. Take what you got, 'cause there's stuff you got, Bob. We're all in this big tragedy of a life together, so shove some timber up your chute, get some matches and let her rip!

BOB. OK. Fine. Sheesh. Fine.

HELEN. Sven! *(Sven returns.)* Remember what we talked about, Sven? *(Sven nods.)* Bob, I give you Sven, the most talented trained Wolf in North America. He will be your faithful companion and lead you to the ends of earth. *(Sven turns to Bob.)*

BOB. No.

HELEN. It's the least I can do.

BOB. But what about the Vegas show?

HELEN. All of a sudden that dream seems a little tacky.

BOB. Hi Sven.

HELEN. I'm sorry I stole your pants. I should never have done that. It was cruel. I am deeply sorry for what I did to you. *(Sven stands between them, watching.)*

BOB. I forgive you, Helen.

HELEN. You do?

BOB. I declare those pants to be your own. *(Beat. Sven sniffles.)*

HELEN. Well, I better be going on my way before I tear up.

BOB. Helen.

HELEN. What's that, Bob?

BOB. Before you ... would you do your RingerTraum for me?

HELEN. Oh, Bob I've never shown it to —

BOB. I want to see it.

HELEN. It's silly without all the parts and —

BOB. We've got Sven and his fleas and we can imagine the rest ...

HELEN. I can't.

BOB. Inspire me. Reveal me. Make me cry.

HELEN. I don't know if I should even — TOTEM! *(Helen's Living Totem is created, but unseen. It is strangely beautiful.)*

BOB. Oh wow.

HELEN. Bob, What animal are you? Which one is your guide on the trail of your life? You are not alone.

BOB. I am not alone. *(The RingerTraum ends. Helen is winded.)*

HELEN. Hoo-ey! That felt amazing to finally share that with someone. Thank you, Bob.

BOB. It was the greatest animal act the world has ever seen.

HELEN. Goodbye, Bob.

BOB. Good luck, Helen. *(Bob and Helen hug.)*

HELEN. Funny, I always say "good luck" to other people too. Never knew whether it actually brought it or not.

BOB. I think it's just a nice thing to say.

HELEN. Remember, Bob, you are not — *(Helen dies in Bob's arms.)*

BOB. "You are not." So said the great animal trainer Helen on this Valentine's Day. Goodbye, Mom. We get one chance. And then we disappear. One chance. And you're in the middle of it. *(Bob puts Helen down over his plaque. Sven licks Helen, maybe eats a toe. Beat.)* Tony? *(Tony runs on.)*

TONY. Yes, Bob?

BOB. Will you rehire me?

TONY. What do you need, Bob?

BOB. We need to light my birth mother on fire.

TONY. Yes, Bob.

BOB. And after that, I would like to put my casino house up for sale.

TONY. OK.

BOB. Sell all of my assets and bring me cash if you wouldn't mind.

TONY. Bob.

BOB. Take a million dollars for yourself and give the rest to the Park Service.

TONY. Bob.

BOB. Just, please, do what I ask. *(Tony exits.)* Sven, look into my eyes. Don't you worry, Sven. You and your fleas won't be left behind. A great future lies ahead for us. *(Sven nods. Scratches. Tony returns with the two Martin Luther Casino bags of money.)* Have a glass of champagne with me, Tony?

TONY. Bob, what are you going to do? *(Blackout.)*

End of Act Four

Interlude Four

A dance about hope.

CHORUS ONE. This is a dance about hope. *(Chorus One dances.)* Thank you.

ACT FIVE

CHORUS ALL. Bob. Act Five.

CHORUS THREE. The rest.

CHORUS ONE. It is said that after Bob left his plaque at Mount Rushmore overflow parking, he was never seen in this country again.

CHORUS TWO. It is said that Tony, who looks a lot like me, found himself in a greater amount of perplexed reflection than he had ever felt for a client and desired to learn more about Bob's past.

CHORUS THREE. Tony searched many pockets of the nation based on the stories Bob had shared. A coffee shop owner recalled a bloody fight with Bob.

BARISTA. That fight we had. It finally turned my life around. Bob helped me find my passion again. I'm having less but more meaningful sex and my coffee shop has become the literary Mecca of Poncha Springs!

CHORUS FOUR. Tony found hundreds of people with an anecdote about Bob. *(A wild flurry of characters past.)*

BONNIE. Bob showed me that my name wasn't the problem. Seeing him in my trunk all those times made me realize it was something deeper, something more profound I should change with my life. And I did. And I'm finally the person I should be. Please, call me Chester.

VERA. Bob taught me what I don't want to be like when I'm grown up. When I am a successful businesswoman, I will always buy cookies for a good cause, I will not lock myself away in a casino, and I will not count on luck to make me happy.

ROULETTE DEALER. Bob got me fired from my roulette job that I was too lazy to leave even though it took my arm. Got me thinking about my master's in social justice and my old desire to spread the message of empowerment. So now I'm the owner of the Malcolm X Bowling Alley in Fresno, California. Get an "X" for Malcolm. That's our slogan.

WAITRESS ONE. Bob never really left my waitress bed in a way.

WAITRESS TWO. Nor mine!

WAITRESS THREE. Nor mine!

WAITRESS FOUR. Nor mine!

WAITRESS ONE. His energy was inspiring.

WAITRESS TWO. Such an amazing kisser.

WAITRESS THREE. Oh wow his lips.

WAITRESS FOUR. I wish I'd glued them to mine with cement.

WAITRESS ONE. Bob convinced me to leave my large husband and spearhead a movement to transform our dilapidated town into a historical and vacation paradise.

WAITRESS TWO. Me too!

WAITRESS THREE. Me too!

WAITRESS FOUR. Not me. But I believe, thanks to Bob, I make the greatest ham and cheese omelet in the tri-valley area.

JAMES. Bob looked after Roberto's bush for years. I think a lot of people fell in love underneath it because of that.

KIM. Bob gave me a pencil. And I made it home.

CAITLYN. Bob was the only one who cared that I didn't pee in my car.

SAGÉ. Bob was like a flea that I can't remember but I feel his bite.

CHORUS THREE. It is said that if Tony were able to speak to the dead, they would have had a lot to say.

CONNOR. Bob helped me grieve. Sometimes you get so tossed up in your own problems it's hard to see beyond your own salad. I think I finally peeked out of the bowl after the day I met him. I'm glad I gave him that ring. That's something I'm proud of.

AMELIA. Bob gave me the strength to pursue my own happiness. It was better to die of exposure and starvation on a raft made of beach trash in the middle of the Pacific Ocean than the slow and painful way my parents had arranged. I wish there was some way I could tell Bob, let him know I didn't stop my journey.

GUNTHER. Bob had a little less hair than I expected. But I could still see it, the animal trainer blood in him. Times two. There are not a lot of people I'd get eaten for. Him and maybe Jimmy Buffett but that's it. I believe there is a beautiful RingerTraum inside of him.

HELEN. Bob allowed me to die in a loved one's arms. And he gave me these pants.

JEANINE. Bob burnt me and it's the best thing he could have done. I am everywhere now. A particle here, a molecule there. You wouldn't believe everything I've bumped against since then. I hope Bob burns himself when the time comes. And I hope he finds a bit of happiness before that. I think a lot of people might have loved him. If they'd given him the chance.

CHORUS TWO. It is said that Tony was so moved he felt compelled to write a short story about Bob and sent it to *Harper's* magazine, which got printed, which got Tony a book deal, which became hugely loved by Oprah Winfrey, which caused the story of Bob to seep into the national consciousness and for Tony to live the immortal life of his dreams.

CHORUS THREE. Other books about Bob appeared, some accurate, some absurdly false, some by people who had never met him. His story was used as lessons for children, for clever bumper stickers, and to prove varying political points of view.

CHORUS ONE. It was hoped by millions that the great celebration and knowledge of Bob's life would compel Bob to appear again.

CHORUS FOUR. He did not.

CHORUS THREE. Most became convinced that Bob was dead. A few came to believe that Tony had invented the entire story, though those people were largely viewed as people not very fun to be around.

CHORUS FOUR. Bob became a legend. Like John Muir. *(All Chorus. Quickly.)*

CHORUS ONE. Harriet Tubman.

CHORUS TWO. Robert Oppenheimer.

CHORUS THREE. Sam Walton.

CHORUS FOUR.Mark Twain.

CHORUS ONE. Eleanor Roosevelt.

CHORUS TWO. Billie Jean King.

CHORUS THREE. Leonard Bernstein.

CHORUS FOUR. Marilyn Monroe.

CHORUS ONE. Duke Kahanamoku.

CHORUS TWO. Chief Seattle.

CHORUS THREE. Bill Gates.

CHORUS FOUR. Cher.

CHORUS ONE. Cesar Chavez.

CHORUS TWO. Jody Williams.

CHORUS THREE. The guy who landed that plane.

CHORUS FOUR. Cher.

CHORUS ONE. And Bob will never know. *(Beat. The Chorus walks away. Chorus Three runs back.)*

CHORUS THREE. Bob was seen one more time.

CHORUS FOUR. It is said.

CHORUS THREE. No, he was. Years ago a young man, Leo, who is a friend of a friend, traveled to Mexico on a backpacking trip to "find himself" and celebrate his sexual attraction to Latin people. On a ride down from Puerto Vallarta to all points south, Leo's bus pulled off the highway to a small rest area known for being the worst in all of Mexico. By a cliff overlooking the Pacific Ocean, Leo saw a small shelter and next to it, a beige Chevy Malibu. This is how Leo met Bob. *(A Chevy Malibu. Bob's legs are sticking out. Leo enters.)*

BOB. *(Under car.)* C'mon, you stupid nozzle. *(Leo adjusts himself to look handsome and alluring)*

LEO. *(In American accent.)* Buenos dias.

BOB. *(A grunt.)* Bwaaah.

LEO. *Me llamo* Leo.

BOB. Hold on a sec, Leo. Just need to twist this one …

LEO. You speak English.

BOB. Correctamundo.

LEO. Are you American? *(Bob emerges from under the Malibu, He is very old, big white beard and wild hair. Maybe dressed in a wolf hide.)*

BOB. Yes, I am.

LEO. *(Disappointed.)* Great.

BOB. You here for the show?

LEO. I'm just going to head back to the —

BOB. No, no! "Whenever someone is in need, put on your shoes!" The great entertainer Shirley Temple said that. *(Over the course of the dialogue, Bob begins to set up little footlights around the Malibu trunk. He wheels out a box on a stand covered by a sheet. Bob changes into a slightly snazzy showman outfit.)*

LEO. I don't really need a —

BOB. Where you from, whippersnapper?

LEO. Small town you've never heard of.

BOB. Try me.

LEO. Mulberry.

BOB. Indiana.

LEO. How did you know?

BOB. One of the best community libraries in the state.

LEO. It's not worth staying in Mulberry for it.

BOB. Great waitresses in Mulberry.

LEO. People think I'm weird there.

BOB. You look a little weird.

LEO. I've known I've been weird since I was nine. I'm OK with it but doesn't seem like Mulberry does. And there's not enough Latin people there.

BOB. So you've set to the road to find your place in the whole hullabaloo of it all.

LEO. I've got a lot of cool ideas, things I could do that could be pretty awesome. I write them down in my journal and translate them into Spanish. I want to be someplace that will believe in me. Chiapas, maybe. I'm a little lost.

BOB. I've felt weird, lost and alone for most of my life. Used to look back at my history and all I'd see are dark moments of failure that stayed vivid and strong. A few little spots poking through like dim little stars that seemed so far away. But, then one day, after years of traveling the continent, I pulled off to this very spot, walked to this very cliff when my trusty dancing wolf began shimmying towards the shore. And there it was: a rectangle of driftwood and plastic and neck pillows all cinched together. On one side, tied to a rope made from a Snickers wrapper, was a glass jar. Filled with water. Its lid shut tight. And I felt Amelia breathing inside of me. And Jeanine next to her. And Connor and Helen and Gunther Roy.

LEO. I don't know those —

BOB. I felt threads coming out of each memory, connecting everything to one another, a bunch of junk from all over the place, bound together into a single raft, keeping me floating above the deep. I felt connected to everything, everywhere, and everyone at the same time. I wanted to capture that. In a case. And never forget that feeling. And I knew what I could do.

LEO. What can you do?

BOB. It'll cost you five hundred pesos.

LEO. That's a lot.

BOB. Leo, you are at the strangest, weirdest attraction at the worst rest stop in all of Mexico. It could change your life. And it includes a shot of whin.

LEO. I have no idea what that is.

BOB. Only one way to find out, Leo. *(Leo gives Bob the money. Bob gives Leo the shot. Bob jumps up on the trunk behind the sheeted object. He wears his ringmaster outfit. The lights change to show lights, bright around the trunk and Bob. Maybe his voice amplified. Music accompanies.)* Ladies, gentlemen, boys, girls, young "weird" Mulberrian lover of the Latinos before me. It has taken me a very long time to build the stamina and strength to perform the act you are about to witness. It may shock you. Thrill and delight you. It may make you cry. Are you willing to accept these risks?

LEO. Uh, yeah?

BOB. Are you ready?

LEO. I don't really know —

BOB. That doesn't sound like ready. Are you ready?

LEO. Yes! Yes, I am ready. I am FRIKKIN' ready! *(Bob pulls back the sheet revealing a flea circus model shaped like the United States of America. There is something about it that's pretty great.)*

BOB. It's Bob's Adventures Across America Flea Circus Spectacular! See my incredible troupe of trained pests reenact one of the wildest collection of life stories ever told. SEE how a fast food employee saves a baby from certain death! SEE how a hobo takes on a savage pack of wolves! Experience The Journey of The Ring, The Curse of the Dollar Bill, The Polaroid Kiss that Changed It All. SEE a flea dance about hardship, love, luck, and hope. *(Bob picks a flea out of Leo's hair.)* AND SEE the tender story of a young man who bravely travels thousands of miles so that he can feel less weird and touch the flesh of a culture he loves. *(Bob places the flea into the case.)* SEE that no matter how far away you feel on the inside, no matter how dark your days can get, you can always take a big step back, look at all those fleas hopping next to you and see that you are NOT ALONE! *(Bob looks down and commands the fleas, or just stands by his circus. Perhaps he silently narrates.)*

CHORUS ONE. It is said that Leo stayed at Bob's for a week, and watched Bob's show several hundred times, and Bob charged him five hundred pesos every time. *(Beat.)*

CHORUS THREE. It is said we like this added conclusion. This final tale of Bob.

CHORUS FOUR. It is said we all like Bob, we think about him a lot, not just because Oprah loved him, but, 'cause, I don't know, we just do.

CHORUS ONE. It is said there are many of us who like uttering those words. We say it to ourselves as we go to sleep in our beds, words that give us comfort and hope in the face of all the discomfort and hopelessness. That we are not alone.

CHORUS TWO. We are not alone.

CHORUS THREE. We are not alone.

CHORUS FOUR. We are not alone. *(Bob with his fleas, content.)*

BOB. I am not alone. I am not alone. I am not alone. *(Blackout.)*

End of Play

PROPERTY LIST

Knife
Instructions
Microphone
Grocery bag
Plaque
Newspapers, sticks, matches
Tissues
Pen
Ring in box
Pillowcase
Bag of trash with water bottles, food scraps, dollar bill, bloody
    shirt, rubber gloves, knife, condoms, 3 books, Snickers wrapper
Pencil
Polaroid camera
Lists
Glass jar
Seed bag
Mail
Coffee mug and pitcher
Cream and sugar
Toast
Butter
Omelet
Plastic change container with a dollar bill
Coffee drink
Matches
Lantern
Muffin wrappers
Flask
Suitcase
Phone booth
Arm
2 glasses of champagne
Roulette wheel
Glass of champagne
Birthday cake
Jar
Sheet-covered object with plaque

Martin Luther Casino bags of money
Chevy Malibu
Footlights
Sheet-covered flea circus on a stand

SOUND EFFECTS

Police siren
Brakes, tires skidding
Distant lion's roar
Wolves
Doorbell
Roulette wheel
RV driving off
Music

NEW PLAYS

★ **CLYBOURNE PARK by Bruce Norris.** WINNER OF THE 2011 PULITZER PRIZE AND 2012 TONY AWARD. Act One takes place in 1959 as community leaders try to stop the sale of a home to a black family. Act Two is set in the same house in the present day as the now predominantly African-American neighborhood battles to hold its ground. "Vital, sharp-witted and ferociously smart." *–NY Times.* "A theatrical treasure…Indisputably, uproariously funny." *–Entertainment Weekly.* [4M, 3W] ISBN: 978-0-8222-2697-0

★ **WATER BY THE SPOONFUL by Quiara Alegría Hudes.** WINNER OF THE 2012 PULITZER PRIZE. A Puerto Rican veteran is surrounded by the North Philadelphia demons he tried to escape in the service. "This is a very funny, warm, and yes uplifting play." *–Hartford Courant.* "The play is a combination poem, prayer and app on how to cope in an age of uncertainty, speed and chaos." *–Variety.* [4M, 3W] ISBN: 978-0-8222-2716-8

★ **RED by John Logan.** WINNER OF THE 2010 TONY AWARD. Mark Rothko has just landed the biggest commission in the history of modern art. But when his young assistant, Ken, gains the confidence to challenge him, Rothko faces the agonizing possibility that his crowning achievement could also become his undoing. "Intense and exciting." *–NY Times.* "Smart, eloquent entertainment." *–New Yorker.* [2M] ISBN: 978-0-8222-2483-9

★ **VENUS IN FUR by David Ives.** Thomas, a beleaguered playwright/director, is desperate to find an actress to play Vanda, the female lead in his adaptation of the classic sadomasochistic tale *Venus in Fur.* "Ninety minutes of good, kinky fun." *–NY Times.* "A fast-paced journey into one man's entrapment by a clever, vengeful female." *–Associated Press.* [1M, 1W] ISBN: 978-0-8222-2603-1

★ **OTHER DESERT CITIES by Jon Robin Baitz.** Brooke returns home to Palm Springs after a six-year absence and announces that she is about to publish a memoir dredging up a pivotal and tragic event in the family's history—a wound they don't want reopened. "Leaves you feeling both moved and gratifyingly sated." *–NY Times.* "A genuine pleasure." *–NY Post.* [2M, 3W] ISBN: 978-0-8222-2605-5

★ **TRIBES by Nina Raine.** Billy was born deaf into a hearing family and adapts brilliantly to his family's unconventional ways, but it's not until he meets Sylvia, a young woman on the brink of deafness, that he finally understands what it means to be understood. "A smart, lively play." *–NY Times.* "[A] bright and boldly provocative drama." *–Associated Press.* [3M, 2W] ISBN: 978-0-8222-2751-9

DRAMATISTS PLAY SERVICE, INC.
440 Park Avenue South, New York, NY 10016 212-683-8960 Fax 212-213-1539
postmaster@dramatists.com www.dramatists.com